BOURINOT'S
RULES
OF ORDER

A manual on the practices and usages of the House of Commons of Canada and on procedure at public assemblies, including meetings of shareholders and directors of companies, political conventions, and other gatherings.

Third Edition

Bourinot's Rules of Order

Sir John George Bourinot
One time Clerk of
the House of Commons

Second Edition
revised by
J. Gordon Dubroy
Second Clerk Assistant:
House of Commons

Third Edition
revised by
Geoffrey H. Stanford

M&S

CANADIAN CATALOGUING IN PUBLICATION DATA

Bourinot, John George, Sir, 1837-1902.
   Bourinot's rules of order

Includes index.
ISBN 0-7710-8334-3 (bound). ISBN 0-7710-8335-1 (pbk.)

1. Canada. Parliament. House of Commons – Rules and practice.
2. Public meetings. I. Stanford, G.H. (Geoffrey Hunt), 1906-   .
II. Dubroy, J. Gordon, 1910-   . III. Title. IV. Title: Rules of order.

JL148.B68 1977   328.71′05   C77-12918-8

Manufactured in Canada by Webcom Limited

McClelland & Stewart Inc.
The Canadian Publishers
481 University Avenue
Toronto, Ontario
M5G 2E9

Contents

Part V: Some Illustrations

PREFACE
TO THE SECOND
EDITION

The first edition of Bourinot's *Rules of Order* was prepared in 1894, a brief period after Confederation. At that time, it would be difficult to discern any major difference in the procedure of the Canadian Commons and that observed by the British House in the late eighteenth century.

In the years since 1900, progressively more and more study has been given to the practice of our House of Commons until today a special committee on procedure is looked upon as a normal proceeding in every session. The latest revision in the standing orders of the House of Commons occurred concurrently with the preparation of this revision.

Much of the material in the first edition remains as valid today as it was in 1894. However, new practices and changing conditions have rendered a portion of the work obsolete or outdated.

In preparing this edition, the arrangement and format of the earlier work have been retained wherever practicable. It is the hope of the editor that this revision will be as widely accepted as was the first edition.

J. Gordon Dubroy
House of Commons
July 1962

PREFACE
TO THE THIRD
EDITION

The previous revision of this work was undertaken to bring it into conformity with the usages which had evolved in the Canadian House of Commons in the course of the current century. The original objective and format remained unchanged: procedures in the Commons arising out of Standing Orders were described and were adapted for use in other deliberative bodies.

A new revision was considered desirable to provide a clearer distinction between the necessarily detailed rules governing the actions of Parliament and those which are acceptable in the meetings of innumerable groups that assemble for the conduct of their private affairs.

It is hoped that in its present form the book will constitute a concise and practical statement of the principles and conventions generally recognized in Canada, and that it may be a useful reference for those who participate in, and particularly those who preside over, assemblies of whatever nature.

G. H. S.
January 1977

INTRODUCTION

A parliamentary system of government began to take shape in Great Britain in the thirteenth century, arising out of Magna Carta and the subsequent great charter or Charter of Liberties. Two processes were at work. The King's feudal court or great council, made up of the barons and principal tenants and composed and summoned at the King's will, possessed certain quasi-legislative and judicial powers and acted largely in an advisory capacity to the King. It was to become the House of Lords, although this name was not applied until the time of Henry VIII. A parallel development was a convocation of other, regarded as lesser, elements of society to consult with the King about financial matters and to perform a limited advisory function in some other areas of administration. This body was to evolve after many years and vicissitudes into the House of Commons, but it was not until the ouster of James II and the "Glorious Revolution" of 1688 that it was able to assert permanent parliamentary sovereignty. An evolutionary process continued in the Commons with various procedural reforms, a gradual extension of the franchise, and a long struggle with the Lords during which the latter's powers were slowly eroded and finally, early in the present century, virtually eliminated.

The impetus to create a true and free parliament (the word parliamentum was first employed in 1239) was to establish a means whereby all levels of society, not merely the nobility, would be empowered to exercise a proper measure of control over the conditions that governed the lives of the common people. The system slowly and painfully developed in Britain to accomplish this end has been a model for the other countries of the Commonwealth and either wholly or in part for other democratic countries throughout the world.

The common law of parliament that governs in Canada is a system of rules and conventions derived directly from the ancient and elaborate system of that great prototype of all legislative assemblies, the Parliament of Great Britain.

Parliamentary institutions were not new or untried in Canada at the time of Confederation, but they were firmly and permanently established by virtue of the British North America Act of 1867 which in its preamble expresses a desire of the federating provinces for "a Constitution similar in Principle to that of the United Kingdom," and expressly states that "there shall be one Parliament for Canada, consisting of the Queen, an Upper House styled the Senate, and the House of Commons." Almost all of the forms, rules and usages of the House of Commons of Great Britain were adopted by the Canadian House by the enactment of a standing order that now reads:

> In all cases not provided for hereafter or by sessional or other orders, the usages and customs of the House of Commons of the United Kingdom of Great Britain and Northern Ireland as in force at the time shall be followed so far as they may be applicable to this House.

With the passage of time some of the forms and mechanics inherited at Confederation have been altered, but the principles involved have remained inviolate. Similarly, provincial legislatures and municipal councils have contrived special rules and forms designed to meet their individual requirements, but basically the practices of these bodies are those of the Canadian House of Commons.

The underlying objective of parliamentary procedure is to establish and maintain conditions which will permit a free and fair interchange of viewpoint on issues regularly brought before the members. As these members represent different parties and local interests, and possess different cultural backgrounds and personal characteristics, it is imperative that the rules be precise and equitable and that they be even-handedly applied under the authority of one whose impartiality and understanding of their intent is beyond dispute.

Jeremy Bentham (1748 – 1832), an English political theorist, set out in his "Essay on Political Tactics" what he considered to be the four fundamental rules or principles to be observed in formulating legislative procedures.

Publicity, says Bentham, is the most important of these principles. All proceedings of Parliament should be open to public scrutiny, and the Members of Parliament, the press, and thereby the public, should receive adequate notice of the hours of sitting and of the business to be considered at any sitting. By means of publicity the support of and assent to laws by the populace at large is obtained.

His next principle of procedure concerns the absolute impartiality of the Speaker or presiding officer. He advocates that there be only one presiding officer, but that there be a substitute available at all times. He goes on to say that the Speaker performs two functions: he is a judge between individual members, and also an agent of the whole assembly. In neither capacity should the Speaker possess any control over the will of the assembly; he should be excluded from the usual field of parliamentary activity. He must not possess a member's rights of proposing motions, of participating in debate, or of voting. He cannot be a judge unless he is above all suspicion of partisanship, and his actions, in turn, must be subject to the control of the assembly.

The third principle concerns the forms of parliamentary procedure. Bentham suggests that proposition, debate, and voting must be separate stages of proceedings and, in the process of obtaining the will of an assembly, those steps must be taken separately. This is to provide for orderly progress and to avoid a confusion of issues; it also implies that a motion, or proposition, should not anticipate debate by including assertions ("whereas" and "in order to" preambles are notable examples) which may or may not be facts or may express opinions that are in essence the purported objective of or reason for the proposal.

Bentham's final principle has to do with freedom of speech. He contends that every member should be allowed to speak as often as he wishes, to prevent an overwhelming of the minority. Most modern legislatures find themselves unable to comply with this dictum; standing orders usually are designed to ensure a fair allocation of time for the expression of opinion, but to place certain limits upon the use of that time to forward the conduct of public business and to avoid an undue subordination of parliamentary rights to an individual or minority.

Parliament, the model for all assemblies, should be, in the words of Winston Churchill, "a strong, easy, flexible instrument of free debate." It attains this status by the willing observance of sensible rules which provide for the orderly consideration of the questions before it, leading to an expression of collective will or opinion. Unanimity cannot always be reached, but procedures which have ensured, and have been seen to ensure, proper deliberation of an issue will lead to acceptance and wider support of the outcome. The meticulous observance of agreed forms is of primary importance in the group conduct of both private and public business, and it will, moreover, help to avoid misunderstandings and friction in the process.

It may not always be possible to reconcile practice with theory, but in effect good procedure is fair play and common sense built on a solid foundation of acknowledged principle. Above all, the rules must not change in the middle of the game.

GLOSSARY

Acclamation – The unopposed election of a candidate for office.

Adjourn – To suspend proceedings to another time and/or place.

Agenda – Literally, things to be done. A list of the items to be dealt with at a meeting, usually arranged in conformity with an agreed order.

Amendment – An alteration of a main motion by substituting, adding or deleting a word or words without materially altering the basic intent of the main motion. An amendment must be proposed by motion and must be seconded.

By-laws – Rules or directives governing the internal affairs of an organization.

Casting Vote – A single vote (usually the prerogative of the Speaker or Chairman) which will determine an issue when there has otherwise been an equality of votes.

Closure – An action to bring debate upon an issue to a conclusion by a specified time, thus forcing a decision on that issue at that time. In Parliament, notice of motion to close a debate must be given by a Minister of the Crown; after notice has been given, the operation of closure is deferred until a subsequent sitting of the House.

Commit – Same as Refer.

Committee of the Whole – The entire body constituting a session resolved into a committee under a chairman other than the Speaker or regular chairman. Its purpose is to facilitate discussion by ameliorating the rules applicable in a formal session.

Constitution – The system of fundamental laws and principles that establishes an institution and prescribes its nature, functions and limits.

Dilatory Motions – Motions that have the effect of postponing consideration of a question for the time being, e.g., motions for reading the orders of the day, for proceeding to another order of business, for the adjournment of the House or the debate.

Division – The separation of a deliberative body into those who support and those who oppose an issue which has been debated and has been brought to a vote. Originally the two groups were physically separated for the purpose of determining the division of opinion; now the determination is made by recording each member's vote as his name is called from the roll.

Ex Officio – By virtue of office or position.

Majority – More than half of the total number of those qualified to comprise an organized body or group, or of those so qualified present at a regularly constituted meeting with a quorum in attendance.

Motion – A substantive, or main, motion is a formal proposal placed before a meeting or deliberative assembly in order that it may be debated to a conclusion. A subsidiary motion is one which affects the disposition of a substantive or main motion, e.g., by bringing it to an immediate vote, by delaying or deferring a decision thereon.

Order – (1) Circumspect behaviour in a meeting which permits the orderly conduct of its business.
(2) An admonition (call to order) by the Speaker or Chairman if the behaviour of the meeting as a whole or of any

individual participant offends the rules, practices or generally accepted usage of the assembly.

(3) An issue (point of order) arising wherein it is claimed that the procedures of the meeting or of an individual participant have departed from or offended against the rules, practices or generally accepted usage of the assembly.

Order Paper – The parliamentary equivalent of an agenda. A list of the things to be done or the business to be transacted in the day's proceedings.

Orders of the Day – The items constituting the business of one day's proceedings, in a pre-determined or agreed order.

Plurality – In a contest between three or more candidates for office, the number of votes received by the winning candidate when such number is less than one-half the total number of votes cast. (See Majority)

Privilege – Questions of privilege relate to all matters affecting the rights and immunities of parliament, or to the position and conduct of members in their representative character. In non-parliamentary bodies, privilege is often regarded as the right of a member to correct inaccuracies or explain circumstances he deems to affect himself detrimentally or reflect improperly upon the organization as a whole. The question of whether or not a matter may be dealt with as one of privilege is to be determined by the Speaker or chairman.

Pro Tem. – For the time being.

Quorum – The number of persons required to be present at a meeting to validate the transaction of its business.

Refer – To direct an issue for consideration by a committee prior to a decision being reached concerning it by the main body.

Resolution – A formal determination made by a body on the basis of a motion, or proposal, duly placed before a regularly constituted meeting of that body for debate and decision.

Scrutineer – One appointed to examine the ballots cast in any voting procedure to determine their admissibility. He may also be assigned the function of teller. In company meetings his duties may include a determination of the number of share-holders present in person or by proxy and, for voting purposes, the number of shares each represents.

Supply – In parliamentary terminology, 'supply' has to do with the moneys requested by the government for its various purposes. The business of supply is dealt with by a committee of the whole House and consists of consideration of any items in main or supplementary estimates; motions to concur in interim supply; motions to reinstate any item in the estimates, and motions to introduce or pass at all stages any bill relating to the estimates.

Teller – One appointed to count votes.

Two-Thirds Vote – A condition imposed when a vote is taken on a major issue whereby approval is contingent on not less than two-thirds of the votes cast being in the affirmative.

Unparliamentary Language – In Parliament no member may speak disrespectfully of Her Majesty, nor any of the Royal Family, nor of the Governor General or other person administering the government of Canada, nor use offensive words against the House of Commons or the Senate or any member thereof. A member may not reflect upon any vote of the House except for the purpose of moving that such a vote be rescinded. In non-parliamentary bodies similar restrictions may be imposed, but the term usually refers to language which would be deemed inappropriate or offensive in normal social relationships.

Ways and Means – In parliamentary terminology, 'ways and means' has to do with the methods to be employed in raising the money required by the government for its various purposes. The business of ways and means is dealt with by a committee of the whole House, and is concerned with budgetary and taxation measures, usually arising from a budget presentation made by a Minister of the Crown.

PART I

THE PARLIAMENTARY
BASIS OF RULES
AND USAGES

Procedure in the Canadian House of Commons is governed by the Standing Orders of the House of Commons issued from time to time under the authority of the Speaker of the House and prepared in printed form by the Queen's Printer for Canada. These Standing Orders set out formally and officially all of the conditions under which the House shall function and rules covering all of the circumstances likely to be encountered in the conduct of the business of the House. They constitute the basis of the Speaker's administration of parliamentary affairs and are his reference in rulings affecting the day-to-day conduct of debate. It is the duty of every new member to acquaint himself with Standing Orders and to govern himself accordingly.

For present purposes a comprehensive outline of Standing Orders would serve little useful purpose, but inasmuch as their essence is translated into rules of procedure for every other type of formal assembly, whether public or private, a review of their main provisions is of interest.

1. Days and Times
The days and times of the sittings of the House of Commons while it is in session are specifically defined in Standing Orders, as are the daily routine, the order of the business to be considered, and the conditions to be observed to effect any variation of normal procedure. Such information is of course necessary to permit the members, coming from all parts of the country, to organize their arrangements for attendance. The actual convoking of a Parliament is the prerogative of the party which, having a predominance of members, forms the government.

2. Election of Speaker

By Section 44 of the British North America Act it is directed that the House of Commons on its first assembling after a general election shall proceed with all practicable speed to elect one of its members to be Speaker. With the Clerk acting as temporary chairman, this is accomplished by a member, usually after prior clearance, moving "that Mr._____, member for the electoral district of _____, do take the Chair of this House as Speaker." The motion being seconded and spoken to, and there being no other proposed, the member so named is called by the House to the Chair. If more than one proposal is made, they are dealt with in order until one member receives a majority vote.

3. Duties of Speaker

The Speaker presides at all meetings of the House of Commons. He does not participate in debate and has no vote except when there has been an equality of votes. It is his duty to preserve order and decorum and, subject to appeal, to decide all questions of order, stating the Standing Order or other authority applicable to the case. A question of privilege (see page 28) raised by a member is taken into consideration by the Speaker either immediately or at a time he appoints.

A member desiring to speak may do so only on recognition by the Speaker, and if in the course of his address a member is called to order by the Speaker he must be seated until the matter is dealt with. Should a member persist in irrelevance or repetition, or employ unparliamentary language, the Speaker may direct him to discontinue his speech. Persistent failure to comply with the Speaker's orders may result in a member's expulsion from the House.

The Speaker is the judge of the propriety of any motion made in the House, and both prior to and at the conclusion of debate on any substantive motion he reads, or has read, the terms of the motion in both official languages. At the conclusion of the debate he puts the question to the House whether it will adopt the motion, and takes the sense of the meeting in either a voice or recorded vote.

4. Deputy Speaker

A Deputy Speaker is also elected at the commencement of every Parliament, to assume all the duties of the Speaker in the latter's absence. Should both the Speaker and Deputy be absent, the Clerk of the House is authorized to act in their stead. The Deputy Speaker takes the Chair of all committees of the whole.

5. Officers of the House

The Clerk of the House is responsible for the safekeeping of all the papers and records of the House, and has control over other Parliamentary clerks and officers under the general supervision of the Speaker and the House as a whole. He provides the Speaker each day with the order of proceedings for that day, and amongst other duties ensures the availability of the legal and other services required by the House.

The Clerk keeps a record of proceedings, but can only recognize the orders of the Chair. When the Speaker has read or proposed a motion to the House, the Clerk enters it in the journal; he takes no note of members' speeches.

The Sergeant-at-Arms has charge of the mace, the symbol of Parliamentary authority, and of the furniture and fittings of the House, and, subject to the orders of the Speaker of the House, directs and controls the constables, messengers and others who service the chamber.

6. Attendance and Quorum

Every member must attend the service of the House unless he is granted leave of absence. Full attendance is rarely achieved, but penalties are imposed when a member's absence is unduly prolonged. At least twenty members must be present, including the Speaker, to permit the House to exercise its powers; this number constitutes a quorum. If at the time of meeting there is not a quorum present the Speaker may adjourn the House until the next sitting day; in doing so he will record the time of adjournment and the names of the members then present.

Should the House be suddenly adjourned due to the absence of a quorum, any question then under consideration will disappear from the order paper for the time being, but may be revived at a subsequent sitting.

A quorum of any committee of the whole is also twenty. A quorum of a standing or special committee is a majority of the members unless otherwise specifically provided.

7. Order of Business

The order of the business to be dealt with by the House each day is rigidly defined in Standing Orders, and this order may not be altered except under special circumstances and by the observance of specified procedures. This is necessary to ensure that members with duties outside the House may be aware of the business being transacted in the House from time to time, or have advance warning of any alteration in the normal procedure.

A motion for reading the Orders of the Day has preference to any motion before the House.

8. Motions

A question to be considered by the House is presented as a motion, which must be duly seconded. It is then read to the assembly by the Speaker, whereupon it is formally entered in the records and is subject to debate. It may then be accepted, amended or negatived. When a motion in either its original or amended form is adopted it becomes a resolution; that is to say it becomes the decision or determination of the House with respect to the matter under consideration. Procedures governing the making, debate, intercession and disposition of motions are laid down in Standing Orders. A motion once made may be withdrawn, but only with the *unanimous* consent of the House.

To avoid misunderstandings and encourage informed consideration, any member may require that the question under consideration be read at any time in the debate, but not so as to interrupt a member while speaking.

If a motion is defeated it may not be re-introduced except in the form of a new proposal sufficiently varied in its terms to constitute a different question, and the House itself may determine whether or not it does in fact constitute a new question.

When a question is under consideration no other main motion may be made, but there are a number of so-called privileged motions which are acceptable, e.g., to amend, to adjourn, to take various actions designed to delay resolution of the issue, to bring debate to a conclusion.

Members may not reflect upon any vote of the House, except for the purpose of moving that such a vote be rescinded. In such a case a member may, after due notice, move "That the order or resolution of the House that is recorded in the 'Votes and Proceedings' of (date) at page _____ and which reads (text of resolution) be rescinded."

9. Amendments

While a substantive motion is under debate any member may, without notice, move to amend it. An amendment is designed to alter or vary the terms of the main motion without materially changing its purport; it may propose that certain words be left out, that certain words be omitted and replaced by others, or that certain words be inserted or added. Every amendment must be strictly relevant to the question being considered. An amendment which would simply negative the effect of the main motion is not acceptable, such an intention being properly fulfilled by merely voting against the motion.

When an amendment to a main motion has been proposed, any member may move to amend such amendment, but only two such amendments may be entertained at the same time. One of the amendments must be disposed of before any new amendment can be entertained. There is, however, no limit to the number of amendments admissible to a question provided this restraint is observed. As an amendment must be relevant to the main motion, so also must an amendment in amendment be relevant to the amendment.

When an amendment to a motion is proposed, the amendment is dealt with first. The Speaker first states the original motion: "Mr. _____, seconded by Mr. _____ moves that, etc." He then puts the amendment: "Mr. _____, seconded by Mr. _____, moved in amendment thereto that, etc." When the motion and amendment have been read the Speaker will say: "Is it the pleasure of the House to adopt the said amendment?"

As far as practicable debate is confined to the proposed amendment. If the amendment is defeated the Speaker will again propose the main question and a debate may ensue thereon, or another amendment may be offered. If the amendment is adopted the Speaker will propose the question in these words: "Is it the pleasure of the House to adopt the main motion (or question) so amended?" The vote at this point may decide the issue, or a member may propose another amendment: "that the main motion, as amended etc., be further amended, etc."

When there are a main motion, an amendment and an amendment thereto, the Speaker will submit the three motions in the reverse of the order in which they were made, following a procedure similar to the one outlined above.

10. Debate

Every member desiring to speak rises in his place and addresses himself to the Speaker. If two or more rise the Speaker calls upon the one who rose first, but a motion may be made that any member who has risen "be now heard" or "do now speak," and such a motion must be put at once without debate.

The first to speak in any debate is the member who has given notice of the motion or bill to be considered. When that item is reached the Speaker calls upon the member to propose the requisite motion; after he has done so the debate begins. The member who seconds the motion has the option of speaking following the mover, but usually he will defer his speech until later in the debate. After the opening speech the Speaker ordinarily recognizes members on either side of the House alternately to distribute the time equitably among the various areas of opinion. Most speeches are restricted to forty minutes.

Members are not referred to by name, but by their constituency or office; "the Honourable Member for (constituency)," "the Honourable Minister of (department)," etc. Speeches are not to be read, but reference may be made to notes. If a member is called to order either by the Speaker or on a point of order raised by another member, he takes his seat while the point is stated. He may then explain and the point of order may be debated, such debate being strictly relevant to the point at issue. The Speaker then gives his decision.

No member may speak twice to a question except to explain a material part of his speech which may have been misquoted or misunderstood. The mover of a substantive motion is, however, allowed a reply, and the Speaker informs the House that the reply of the mover of the original motion closes the debate.

Not all motions are debatable, those debatable and those not debatable being clearly set out in Standing Orders. As a rough generality, substantive issues on which there will obviously be varying opinions are open to debate, while those of a procedural nature are not.

The Speaker does not take part in any debate before the House, but in the event of an equality of voices he gives a casting vote.

11. Special Motions

There is a class of so-called "dilatory" motions which may be used to postpone a question for the time being. Motions for reading the orders of the day, for proceeding to another order of business, or for the adjournment of debate or the House have the effect of delaying or superseding the consideration of a question, and they must be decided forthwith without debate or amendment. Such motions cannot, of course, be made if the House has already decided that the question be now put or that a bill be now read a second or third time.

A motion to adjourn is always in order, but a simple motion to adjourn the House should not be confused with a motion to adjourn the House for the purpose of discussing a specific matter of urgent public importance. In the latter, a motion may be introduced after the daily introductory procedures have been observed at the outset of a sitting, the member desiring to do so asking leave of the House for that purpose and handing a written statement of the matter to be discussed to the Speaker, who possesses the right to decide, without debate, whether the matter warrants setting aside the regular business of the House. He must satisfy himself that it relates to a genuine emergency calling for immediate and urgent consideration, that it does not anticipate future regular business nor revive discussion of issues already dealt with, and that it does not raise a question of privilege. These safeguards are imposed to provide against misuse of the procedure and to ensure that it is employed to achieve a definite and acceptable end without in any way infringing upon the rights and privileges of the House or deflecting it unduly from the proper conduct of its affairs.

If the Speaker decides that the motion to adjourn is acceptable and the House does not object, the member concerned moves "That the House do now adjourn." Such a motion can be superseded by a motion to proceed to the orders of the day, or it may be withdrawn by consent of the House. Debate on any such motion expires upon the termination of a sitting.

A motion designated "the previous question" is made in the words "That this question be now put." The main object of this motion is to prevent the proposing of an amendment and thus force a direct vote on the main question. The motion requires a seconder, but it cannot be moved or seconded by a member who has spoken on the main question. It can be debated but it cannot be amended. If resolved in the affirmative the question must be put forthwith on the main motion. If defeated, the main motion may not be put at that time, but it may be revived on a future day. The "previous question" thus can be a device to avoid coming to a decision on a subject under discussion, although this end can be better achieved by moving "That the House proceed to the next order of business," which must be decided forthwith without debate.

A motion for the previous question and a motion to which it has been proposed may both be superseded by a motion to adjourn the House or one to proceed to another order of business. Both of these motions must be decided at once without amendment or debate. When the House adjourns daily at the specified hour, without a question being put, a motion for the previous question does not lapse, but debate thereon may carry over from day to day.

The most decisive action to terminate debate is closure. Having given previous notice, a Minister of the Crown may, immediately before an adjourned debate on an issue is to be resumed, move that the debate shall not be further adjourned or that further consideration of a matter shall not be further postponed, and his motion must be decided without debate or amendment. If his motion carries, a time limit is imposed on speeches and the question to which it applies must be decided by the conclusion of that sitting. It is to be noted that responsibility for closure rests with a Minister of the Crown and that notice is required so that the actual termination of debate is not forced until a later sitting of the House.

12. Putting the Question

Debate on a question closes when no member rises to speak, or it may be ended by the Speaker pursuant to a standing order or a directive of the House. The Speaker then puts the question by saying "The question is as follows: Mr. _____ seconded by Mr. _____ moved _____." After reading the motion he says "those in favour of the motion will please say yea," and after a pause to allow the supporters to answer he continues "Those opposed to the motion will please say nay."

On the evidence of the voices the Speaker will then say "In my opinion the yeas (or nays) have it," thus declaring the motion carried or lost. If the House does not agree with his decision a division may be called, a process originally calling for the physical separation of those for and against an issue put to the vote. Now, when the members have been called in for a recorded division the Speaker again puts the question and says "Those in favour of the motion will please rise." As each member stands one of the clerk's assistants calls out his name and the clerk, who has before him a list of all the names, places a mark against each name as it is called. A similar procedure then follows for those opposed to the motion. The clerk counts the votes on both sides and reports the result to the Speaker, who then declares the motion either carried or lost. In a division the yeas and nays are not entered in the minutes unless demanded by five members.

In case of an equality of votes the Speaker gives a casting vote, and then only in accordance with the principle that his vote is not to be construed as an expression of opinion upon the merits of the question. According to tradition the Speaker endeavours to vote in such a way as to provide a further opportunity to consider the question, and any reasons stated by him are entered in the record.

Members may not enter, leave or cross the House when the Speaker is putting a question, and if a member is not present when the question is put he cannot have his vote recorded. While a member is expected to record his vote in every case, there is nothing to oblige him to do so. Should a member inadvertently vote contrary to his intention, he cannot correct his mistake and his vote must remain as first recorded. There must be no debate on a question after it has been fully put by the Speaker, i.e., after he has taken the affirmative and negative votes.

13. Order

It is the right and duty of every member to bring to the attention of the Speaker any deviation or departure from the rules or ordinary procedure of the House, and any such point of order must be clearly and succinctly stated. When the Speaker or any other member rises on a point of order the member who has the floor must resume his seat until the matter is dealt with. A point of order should be raised when the alleged irregularity occurs; it is not acceptable if other proceedings have intervened.

The Speaker may permit debate on a question of order before giving his decision, but such debate must be strictly relevant to the point at issue. When the Speaker feels that he has had an adequate expression he terminates the debate and gives his ruling, stating the Standing Order or authority applicable to the case. No debate is allowed on the ruling, but the Speaker's decision is subject to an appeal to the House, without debate. Any member may rise and state: "Mr. Speaker, I respectfully appeal to the House from your ruling." The Speaker's response is "The House has heard the ruling of the Chair. The question is: Shall the ruling of the chair be sustained? Those in favour will please say yea." He follows this with a request for the negative vote and ordinarily will declare that the yeas have it. At this stage any five members may rise and demand a recorded vote, which will be taken in the usual way and the Speaker will then declare his ruling sustained or not sustained as the case may be.

Sometimes a member will rise on a so-called point of order to refute or dispute a statement by a member who has the floor. The Speaker will simply inform him that his is not a point of order and the debate proceeds.

14. Privilege

Questions of privilege cover a wide range, but in general they have to do with matters affecting the rights and immunities of the House collectively or with the position and conduct of members in their representative character. A breach of privilege is, in effect, a wilful disregard by a member or any other person of the dignity and lawful authority of Parliament.

A question of privilege should be raised after prayers and before the House has taken up the orders of the day. The business of the House will be interrupted for such a question only in urgent cases requiring immediate action.

A genuine question of privilege is a matter presented as a motion, whereupon the House may impose a penalty or apply a remedy. The Speaker decides whether or not there has in fact been a breach of privilege, but his decision may be challenged by an appeal to the House. When it has been established that a breach of privilege has occurred the matter is ordinarily referred to the Committee on Privileges and Elections, where it is considered and a report made back to the House for action thereon.

If a motion is to be made concerning the conduct of a member or his election or his right to hold his seat, due notice is given so that he may be present in the House to reply to the charge. When he has made his statement he withdraws until the matter is dealt with.

Not infrequently members rise on so-called questions of privilege to correct reports of their speeches or to comment on allegedly inaccurate statements in the news media, but these properly are personal explanations, not matters of privilege, and are allowed only by the indulgence of the House. A member sometimes will raise as a question of privilege something that is, at most, merely a question of order.

15. Decorum

It is the Speaker's duty to preserve order and decorum in the House and to deal promptly and fairly with any untoward incident that may arise. In deciding a point of order or practice he states the Standing Order or other authority applicable to the case; no debate is permitted on any such decision, and no such decision is subject to an appeal to the House. A member called to order for breach of parliamentary decorum is expected to comply at once with any directive given by the Speaker, withdrawing any offensive words or apologizing for any inadvertent infringement of the rules and customs of the House. If he does not do so and continues with offensive, irrelevant or repetitious remarks the Speaker may name him for disregarding the authority of the Chair and submit his conduct to the judgement of the House. In naming a member the Speaker uses the words "Mr. ____, member for ____, I have to name you for disregarding the authority of the Chair."

In extreme cases the leader of the House may move that the offending member be suspended from the House for one or more sittings, and such a motion must be decided forthwith without amendment or debate. Should he then not comply voluntarily the Speaker directs the Sergeant-at-Arms to escort him from the chamber.

It is provided that when a member is speaking no member shall pass between him and the Chair, nor interrupt him except to raise a point of order.

16. Questions

Questions may be placed on the order paper seeking information from Ministers of the Crown on matters of public concern, and from other members relating to matters connected with the business of the House. In putting and answering questions no argument or opinion is to be offered, and any facts stated must be wholly relevant to the question at issue. A question may not contain charges which the questioner is not prepared to substantiate, and must not seek solutions to abstract legal cases. A question cannot be made the pretext for a debate, and when a question has been fully answered it cannot be renewed.

A member may require an oral answer to a question placed on the order paper. There is also provision for oral questions, without notice, before the orders of the day are called, although this is considered a courtesy to enable urgent and important matters to be dealt with. Such questions, and the answers, are to be concise, and no debate is permitted. The Minister interrogated may reply at once, or he may ask that the usual notice be given, or he may simply announce that he will reply at the next or a subsequent sitting.

17. Committees of the Whole House

Parliament may resolve itself into a Committee of the Whole House for the consideration of a bill or other substantial issue when it is desirable to permit freer and fuller consideration than would be possible in a formal sitting of the House.

When an order of the day is read for the House to go into a committee of the whole or when it is ordered that a bill or any item in the main or supplementary estimates be considered in a committee of the whole, the Speaker leaves the chair without any question being put. This action is normally the outcome of prior notice to the effect "That this House do go into committee of the whole at its next sitting to consider a certain proposed resolution respecting ____ (subject)."

A member is elected at the commencement of every Parliament to serve as Deputy Speaker and Chairman of Committees, and such member takes the chair of all committees of the whole. In the absence of such Deputy Speaker and Chairman of Committees when the House resolves itself into a committee of the whole, the Speaker, before leaving the Chair, may appoint any member as chairman, although the House itself may appoint a Deputy Chairman and Assistant Deputy Chairman of Committees to serve throughout the session. The chairman maintains order in committees of the whole, deciding all questions of order subject to an appeal to the Speaker, but disorder in a committee must be reported to and dealt with by the House itself.

As far as may be applicable the Standing Orders of the House are observed in committees of the whole House, the exceptions being that motions are not seconded, members may speak more than once to the same question, and no member other than the Prime Minister and the leader of the opposition may speak for longer than twenty minutes. Speeches must be strictly relevant to the issue under consideration and a committee may deal with only such matters as have been referred to it. The committee is not at liberty to go beyond its terms of reference, and an amendment cannot be used to import an argument that would be irrelevant to the main question.

In committees of the whole debate is carried on as in the House itself, and a majority decision rules. In the case of an equality of votes the chairman has a casting vote. If a division is required, the votes on each side are counted and reported to the chairman, who declares the motion carried or lost, but names are not recorded.

When the matters referred to a committee of the whole have been fully dealt with the chairman is directed to report the outcome to the House, and until that is done the House may not refer to the question at issue or the committee's deliberations. Whenever a resolution of a committee of the whole is reported to the House a motion to concur in it must be put forthwith and decided without debate or amendment.

A committee of the whole may consider a matter in part and

report progress to the House, being reconstituted to continue its work when the order for the committee is again read. A motion to "report progress and ask leave to sit again" is equivalent to a motion to adjourn debate and may be used merely to defer discussion of a bill or other issue.

Should a member wish to have a question entirely set aside he may move that the chairman leave the chair, and such a motion is always in order, takes precedence of any other motion, and is not debatable. If resolved in the affirmative the chairman at once leaves the chair and, as no report can be made to the House, the bill or question disappears from the order paper. It can be restored only by a motion made after due notice.

18. Committee of Supply
At the beginning of each session a committee of supply is appointed to consider the "supply" to be granted to Her Majesty. The sole function of this committee is to grant, reduce or refuse the moneys requested by the government. On a request of the Governor General, made on the advice of the ministry, proposed expenditures are reviewed by the committee of supply and the committee's recommendations are approved by the House and enacted by Parliament. The committee may not increase a proposed grant nor any part thereof nor attach any conditions or expression of opinion to its vote, nor may it change the destination of a grant or any part thereof. However, an amendment to reduce a grant or any part of it is always in order.

Supply votes are submitted in the form: "That a sum not exceeding ____ be granted to Her Majesty for (department or service) for the year ending (date)." The motion is made by the minister for whose department or service the money is to be provided, and is subject to amendment.

The rules that obtain in other committees of the whole apply to the committee of supply. Debate must be strictly relevant to the proposed grant under consideration; when a decision has been reached on a proposal it is irregular to refer back to the matter; it is improper to discuss any proposal before it has been formally presented.

There are in addition Standing Orders creating special conditions to apply when Parliament is engaged in the business of supply, the general intent of which is to ensure that questions of funding are made available for wide and meticulous scrutiny. On certain allotted days, for example, opposition members may introduce motions relating to any matter within the jurisdiction of the Parliament of Canada, subject only to the general rules of the House.

19. Committee of Ways and Means

The function of the committee of ways and means, another committee of the whole House, is to consider methods for raising the supply (moneys) to be granted to Her Majesty. Budgeting and taxation measures originate in this committee upon a motion of a Minister of the Crown. Proposals so initiated may not be amended to increase the amount or extend the incidence of tax impositions.

When an order of the day is designated at the request of a Minister of the Crown for the consideration of a ways and means motion for the purpose of a budget presentation, the motion proposed is "That this House approves in general the budgetary policy of the Government."

Rules that obtain in other committees of the whole House apply equally to the committee of ways and means.

20. Standing and Special Committees

Committees are established to facilitate the conduct of the business of Parliament. At the beginning of each session a striking committee of seven members is appointed to prepare and report lists of members to compose various standing committees, currently eighteen in number, such as a committee on agriculture, on external affairs and national defence, on national resources and public works, etc. When the recommendations of the striking committee are approved by the House such committees continue from session to session within a Parliament, with such adjustments of personnel as may be required from time to time.

Standing committees are empowered to examine and enquire into all matters referred to them by the House and to report from time to time. Unless contrarily ordered by the House they may send for persons, papers and records, sit while the House is sitting or while it stands adjourned, publish papers and records, summon witnesses, and delegate any or all of their powers except the power to report directly to the House.

The House may also from time to time appoint special committees of not more than fifteen members for the discharge of designated functions.

Each committee elects its own chairman and vice-chairman who shall, while in the chair, maintain order and decide all questions of order subject to an appeal to the committee. Disorder in a committee, however, can be censured only by the House on receiving a report thereof. The Standing Orders of the House are to be observed as far as may be applicable, except orders relating to the seconding of motions, limiting the number of times of speaking and the length of speeches.

A majority of the members of a standing or special committee constitutes a quorum and a quorum is required whenever a vote, resolution or other decision is taken.

A member of the House who is not a member of a specific standing or special committee may nevertheless take part in its public proceedings, but he cannot be counted in the determination of a quorum nor may he vote or move any motion.

21. Petitions
A petition to the House may be presented by a member at any time during a sitting by filing it with the clerk during routine proceedings. It may be written or printed and it must be endorsed with the signature of the member presenting the petition. When there are three or more petitioners the signatures of at least three are required. Only a member may present a petition, but he may do so on behalf of a constituent or constituents provided he assumes full responsibility in the matter. The form of the actual petition is dictated by usage to ensure the avoidance of misconstruction of its terms or of improper reflection upon the Queen or her representative in Canada, or on the actions of Parliament or any of its committees, or on the courts of justice.

On presenting a petition no debate concerning it is allowed, but the next day the clerk tables a report of the clerk of petitions on the petition presented and, provided it contains no improper matter and generally conforms with the Standing Orders and practices of the House, it is deemed to be read and received and is so recorded. No debate is permitted on the report, but a petition referred to therein may be read by the clerk; if it complains of a personal grievance requiring a prompt remedy, the matter may be brought into immediate discussion.

22. Public Bills

Public bills may originate in either the House of Commons or the Senate, but whenever they involve an expenditure of public money or the imposition of any taxation they must be initiated in the House of Commons. Proceedings on a money or taxation bill are initiated by a resolution in a committee of the whole, including the committees of supply and ways and means.

Every bill is introduced upon motion for leave, specifying the title of the bill. It must not be introduced in blank or in an imperfect shape, and a motion for leave to introduce it must be decided without debate or amendment, except that a member moving for such leave may give a succinct explanation of the provisions of the bill.

When any bill is duly presented by a member the question "That this bill be read a first time and be printed" is to be decided without debate or amendment. Every bill must receive three separate readings before it can be passed, except that on urgent or extraordinary occasions a bill may be read twice or thrice, or advanced two or more stages, in one day. All bills must be printed in both the English and French languages before the second reading. It must be read twice and referred to a committee before any amendment can be offered. Ordinarily it will be referred to the appropriate standing committee, but it may be directed to a special committee or a joint committee of the House and Senate. A bill dealing with supply or ways and means (a money bill) is referred to a committee of the whole House.

At the committee stage the bill is considered clause by clause and is subject to amendment. Amendments to clauses of a bill must be relevant to the subject-matter and must not be outside the scope of the particular clause under consideration. They must be consistent with the provisions of the bill as agreed upon to that point by the committee, and an amendment to delete a clause is improper, since the same effect can be achieved by voting against it.

At the conclusion of its consideration the committee reports to the House and its report, whether containing amendments or not, is received. Forty-eight hours must then elapse, unless otherwise ordered by the House, before the report stage of any bill can be taken into consideration. If the report is from a committee of the whole, it must be received and at once disposed of without amendment or debate. There is, however, provision for notice being given in the interim of a motion to amend, debate, insert or restore any clause in a bill, and such a motion becomes subject to debate and amendment. When a bill has been amended or there has been debate on a proposed amendment at the report stage it is set down for third reading and passage at the next sitting of the House. If no amendment is proposed at the report stage, and in the case of bills reported from a committee of the whole, a motion "That the bill be now read a third time and passed" may be made at the same sitting. When proceedings at the report stage on any bill have been concluded a motion "That the bill, as amended, be concurred in" or "That the bill be concurred in" is put and forthwith disposed of without amendment or debate.

A Minister of the Crown may, usually after having secured the assent of the other parties represented in the House, propose an allotment of days or hours for the proceedings at any stage of the passing of a public bill.

When a bill has received third reading and passed it is sent to the Senate with a request for concurrence. A bill must be presented to the Governor General for Royal Assent before it can become law.

23. Private Bills

Private bills are distinguished from public bills in that they relate directly to the affairs of private persons or of corporate entities and not to matters of general public policy or to the community at large. A petition for the introduction of such a bill must be received by the House within the first six weeks of the session. The petition is examined by the chief clerk of private bills, who also is responsible for seeing that proposed bills, before they are printed, are drawn in accordance with the orders and practices of the House. A fee is assessed for the introduction of a private bill, the costs of printing must be met, and there is a scale of additional charges covering various eventualities.

Generally speaking the Standing Orders applicable to public bills apply to private bills, but there are minor procedural variations. After second reading a private bill is referred to the appropriate standing committee, which is empowered to call in the interested parties to establish and/or clarify the facts upon which the bill is founded. This is an important step, as private bills are usually based on considerations which take no account of public policy and the House must be made aware of proposed provisions of the bill which may be deemed to be contrary to such policy. The committee's decision is by majority vote, including that of the chairman, who also has a casting vote if the votes are equal, and the committee's findings are reported to the House. Private bills amended in committee may be reprinted by order of the committee and at the expense of the promoter of the bill.

In addition to the procedures initiated and taken in the House, all applications to Parliament for private bills of any nature whatsoever must be advertised by a notice published in the Canada Gazette, with similar notice to be published in newspapers in the principal territories in which the effects of the bill, if passed, would be manifest.

Private bills may originate in either the House of Commons or the Senate, and when the Speaker informs the House that a private bill has been brought from the Senate the bill is deemed to have been read a first time and is ordered for a second reading and reference to a standing committee at the next sitting of the House.

24. Reports

All business transacted in each daily sitting of the House is recorded in Votes and Proceedings, and a verbatim account of the proceedings is reported in Hansard.

PART II

RULES AND USAGES
FOR ASSEMBLIES
GENERALLY

25. Rules Necessary

In every assembly of people brought together for the purpose of considering matters of common interest it is essential that there be clear and well understood rules under which the proceedings are to be conducted. These may be the formal Standing Orders of the House of Commons discussed briefly in the last chapter, or they may be an abbreviated and simplified system adapted to the purposes of relatively small and informal bodies. All rules are, however, based on the usages of Parliament, and their function, in bodies large or small, is to ensure that proper opportunity is afforded to all concerned for an expression of opinion, that the rights of a minority are respected, that clear decisions or conclusions are reached on the issues raised on the basis of a free majority vote, and to the extent possible that proceedings are governed by an assessment of the issues rather than by personality factors.

Government bodies, public companies and most important organizations are in essential ways governed by statutes or by their respective constitutions or charters of existence. Such statutory enactments cannot be changed at the will of the body they govern, but only by the superior legislative authority that enacted them. Generally speaking, all bodies do possess, however, either expressly or by implication, the right to make such rules, regulations and by-laws as may be necessary to their existence and usefulness. It is obviously essential that any body intending to have a continuous existence should at the earliest stage prepare and confirm the rules under which it is to function.

26. Changing the Rules

Should it at any time become necessary or advisable to change the rules, precautions must be taken to avoid haphazard action. It is usual to refer suggested alterations to a committee for detailed consideration, and when all of the changes have been worked out notice should be given at one meeting of the organization that at the next or a subsequent meeting a motion will be introduced to give effect to the proposed changes. Before the meeting at which such a motion is to be put, it is advisable that every active member be advised of the changes intended so that he may come to the meeting fully informed and hence prepared to act appropriately.

The procedure to be followed in altering the rules is equally applicable to any innovation, such as an enlargement of objectives, changes in membership qualifications or fees, etc., and no changes should be given effect until a time subsequent to that at which they were approved.

27. Suspension of Rules

Occasionally it may be necessary to suspend certain rules, but this should be allowed to occur only in cases of extreme urgency, usually when time is a dominant factor or when it becomes expedient to deal with an extraordinary item not provided for in routine business. The suspension of a rule for a specific purpose should be on motion and it is customary to insist upon unanimous assent. When the purposes for which a suspension was made have been achieved, the rule returns to full force and effect. For instance, if urgency has not permitted giving the number of days' notice of a meeting called for in the by-laws, the first business of such a meeting should be the passage of a motion suspending the rule for the purposes of that particular meeting and declaring the meeting duly called and regularly constituted. Thereafter the rule again becomes operative.

28. Assemblies

The business of every legislative and deliberative assembly, every municipal council, association, ecclesiastical assembly and synod, association and every other body of people organized to gather together for agreed objects, is transacted at a "meeting," "sitting," or "session." A "meeting" comprises the time between the assembling or convening of a body until the close of its proceedings or an adjournment. A "sitting" is the word applied to a daily meeting of Parliament or of any other important body whose affairs are conducted in a regular way over a period of time. A "session" properly means the duration of the several meetings or sittings of a legislative or other deliberative body which assembles at a fixed time and from day to day or on a specified sequence of days, and finally after a week, month, or longer period comes to a close by dissolution, prorogation or other formal action. Many other bodies will meet once a week, a month, or even annually for the transaction of their business, in which event the word "meeting" is practically synonymous with "session." If any such meeting must be adjourned until another day to complete consideration of the business for which it was convoked, the next meeting is in effect the same meeting and it should be conducted with the same agenda, as if there had been no break in the proceedings.

29. Notice of Meetings
Every person entitled to attend a meeting must be informed in advance of the day, time and place at which the meeting is to be held. Whether meetings are held irregularly, or more or less regularly but not necessarily always on the same day or time or at the same place, such person should receive a notice with all necessary information well in advance of the meeting date, and this of course becomes particularly important when those qualified to attend live at some distance from the place of assembly.

In the case of a session, or of a series of meetings to be held consecutively within a specified period, one notice will usually suffice, provided it contains all of the information necessary to permit those concerned to organize their time and arrange to attend the various sittings.

With notices of meetings it is usual, and beneficial, to include information about the nature of the business to be dealt with. Included, if practicable, should be copies of reports or other supporting papers relating to the matters to be considered, to permit prior thought being given to the issues.

30. The Presiding Officer
Every body of people assembled for the purpose of discussion, deliberation, making decisions and promoting certain objects must be presided over by one individual – the chairman. This

individual, corresponding broadly with the Speaker of the House of Commons, may be recognized by various titles according to the usage, rule or law that governs the various assemblies, but his rights, duties and responsibilities are in all cases similar. "President" is the term generally employed for persons appointed or elected for a fixed period as the presiding officers of societies, associations, corporate bodies and the like. "Mayor," "warden" and "reeve" are titles applied to those heading municipal or other territorial councils, while fraternal and religious organizations have designations peculiar to themselves.

While a meeting is in progress all remarks are to be addressed to the presiding officer by his appropriate title: Mr. Mayor, Mr. President, etc., although in the absence of accepted usage to the contrary it is correct to address the occupant of the chair simply as Mr. Chairman, for however named he (or she) is simply a presiding officer for the purposes of the meeting and in the general sense of the common law that governs all assemblies.

31. Absence of Presiding Officer

It is usual, and good, practice to elect or appoint a deputy (or vice-)chairman or vice-president or other officer who shall be qualified and automatically entitled to take the place of the regular presiding officer in the event of the latter's temporary absence. While occupying the chair he shall possess all the rights, duties and responsibilities of the officer he is temporarily replacing.

Should circumstances arise in which both the regular presiding officer and his deputy are unavoidably absent, the assembly may appoint a chairman *pro tem.*, This is done on motion of any member "That Mr. ____ do now take the chair." If the regular presiding officer appears in the course of a meeting at which the chair is occupied by a temporary appointee, the latter concludes the item of business under consideration, then surrenders the chair to its regular occupant.

32. Duties of Chairman

The chairman, however named, occupies an important position in any assembly. He calls the meeting to order to begin the proceedings, announces the items of business in the order in which they appear on the agenda, reads the motions to the meeting as they are put so that they may be formally debated, submits motions or other proposals for the final decision of the meeting or assembly by their vote or other expression, and having assembled the sense of the meeting announces that the motion or proposal has been carried or lost. He will adjourn the meeting if further consecutive meetings are to be held, or finally close it if all the purposes of the present meeting have been fulfilled.

He must decide, subject to appeal, all questions of order and procedure, and he must at all times preserve that order and decorum essential to calm deliberation, effective employment of the available time, and general agreement that fair and equitable processes have led to acceptable conclusions.

In large, formal meetings the chairman officiates to ensure the efficient conduct of the business before the assembly without himself participating in debate. He remains objective and impartial, acting strictly as an umpire of proceedings, such removal from active participation being necessary in view of the authority he possesses to regulate the conduct of the gathering and his obligation to see that conflicting opinion receives equal expression. In these circumstances the chairman has no vote, but he may exercise a deciding or casting vote if the votes are otherwise equal.

In less formal gatherings and in committees the chairman, while discharging all of the usual functions in conducting the proceedings, enjoys the same right as any other member to participate in discussion and to vote on any issue. However, should a chairman himself wish to propose a motion, he should surrender the chair to the vice-chairman (or to anyone else if the latter is not present) and he should not resume the chair until his motion has been fully disposed of.

Anyone assuming a chairman's duties should:

(a) have reasonable assurance that he has the time and inclination to play the part;

(b) have a sufficient working knowledge of the rules of procedure to permit him to discharge his duties with confidence and to the satisfaction of his associates;

(c) be familiar with the constitution, by-laws, rules and usages of the organization he serves: and

(d) possess qualities of tactful decisiveness conducive to effective and controlled progress.

A principal officer may of course have many duties to perform in addition to those involved in the active conduct of meetings. He should interest himself in preparations for meetings and be assured that all needful material such as reports are available or have been distributed. Similarly he should see that all decisions for action agreed to at meetings of the group are given effect precisely in accordance with such decisions and any related instruction. He is customarily the signatory of official papers produced on his organization's behalf and will sometimes be called upon to act as his organization's representative and spokesman in contacts with other bodies and with the press.

33. Choosing the Presiding Officer

In most cases an organization's principal officer will be chosen in accordance with applicable laws or specific procedures detailed in the body's constitution or by-laws, or sometimes even with long-accepted custom. An officer so chosen will then automatically preside at assemblies of the members unless specific alternate arrangements are made.

In the event of an assembly being brought together without a designated leader, one of the earliest actions should be the choice of someone to preside. It is proper in these circumstances for anyone who has taken some part in bringing the group together to call for the nomination of a chairman, a chairman *pro tem.,* or of such other officer or officers, permanent or temporary, as may suit the circumstances. Upon nomination being made and seconded, it is voted upon and usually the nominee will be found readily acceptable. If two or more nominees are proposed a vote is taken on each in the order in which they were proposed, i.e., the first name is voted upon, and if rejected, the second name, and so forth. If the votes are equal the motion is deemed to be lost and the next name is proposed for a decision.

If a meeting is convoked for a specific purpose the duties of the individual chosen to preside are deemed to be fully discharged at the conclusion of that meeting or any adjournment thereof, or whenever such purpose has been fully achieved. A chairman chosen *pro tem.* at the inaugural meeting of a body intending to have a continuing existence continues to act until such time as regular procedures have been set up and a permanent presiding officer has been elected in accordance therewith.

By-laws or regulations may set the term of a presiding officer and conditions may be established to provide that the office cannot be held by the same individual for more than a specified number of successive terms.

34. Quorum
A quorum is the minimum number of persons who must be present to validate the transaction of business. In legislative bodies a quorum is established by statute or standing orders and is usually many less than the total number of members of such bodies. Other organizations may set the number to comprise a quorum by by-law or regulation. If no provision is made, a quorum shall be a majority of the total number of members of a body. It is good practice to have the number of a quorum clearly fixed, particularly for large groups; the attendance of four of a committee of six may usually be expected, whereas more than half of a group of a hundred may very well not appear.

The official business of a body may not be transacted in the absence of a quorum. Should members leave in the course of a meeting that has begun with a quorum, proceedings should cease at the point at which the number attending falls below that required, the chairman at this point being faced with the necessity of adjourning the meeting to a later date if items remain on the agenda that still require attention. (There is an informal procedure in this situation wherein interim decisions may be reached, but they cannot be regarded as the official decisions of the body nor be acted upon until they have been ratified at a subsequent meeting with a quorum present.)

The importance placed upon the quorum is due to the need to avoid any appearance of action by a minority which might commit the whole group without its assent or the opportunity to advance dissenting opinion.

35. Order of Business
An order of business, or agenda, should be prepared in advance of every meeting. It will ordinarily be the duty of the secretary, or of such other officer as may discharge secretarial duties, to compile a list of the items to be dealt with, to ensure that it is in the hands of the officer who is to preside, before the meeting begins, and it is desirable also that copies be made available for all in attendance. The order of the items of business will usually follow an accustomed pattern, beginning with the reading of the minutes of the

preceding meeting, then reports, followed by pending business and new business in a convenient arrangement.

The business should be called item by item by the chairman, following the order in which they appear on the agenda. He should not depart from the pre-arranged order unless he has a strong reason for doing so, such as the delayed attendance of a member who may be important to the discussion. A change in the order of business should in any event be made only after establishing that the meeting as a whole does not object.

If an agenda has been properly prepared in advance and all in attendance know at the outset the items it contains, conduct of the meeting will be facilitated. Some foreknowledge will induce forethought, the introduction of irrelevancies will be discouraged, and the unnecessary anticipation of questions set down for later consideration will be avoided.

While there is no rule governing the introduction at a meeting of new questions not contained in the prepared agenda, this is a matter of some importance and the chairman should be prepared to deal with the situation if it arises. At a formal meeting he would be within his rights to decline to admit such questions for consideration, as members have had no prior advice that they would be raised and they may be inadequately informed to deal with them properly. On the other hand, at smaller or committee meetings the chairman might properly permit consideration of a new issue if time permits and *provided* objection is not taken to its introduction.

36. Motions

A motion is a proposal placed before a meeting, and properly all decisions recorded as being those of the meeting should be on the basis of motions either adopted or defeated. A motion that has been adopted becomes a resolution of the meeting. There should be only one main or substantive motion before a meeting at any one time.

To the extent possible a motion should be worded in affirmative terms and it should express fully and unambiguously the intent of the mover. It should not be preceded by a preamble ("Whereas . . ." or "In order to . . ."), since these represent opinions which are arguable or make statements which may or may not be factual. A motion is made by a member securing the recognition of the chairman, rising and, addressing the chairman, simply stating "I move that. . . ." An important motion, or one containing a number of considerations, should be prepared in writing and given to the chairman, preferably in advance of the meeting. All main motions should be seconded by another member making a statement to that effect. Unless seconded such a motion is not open to consideration.

When seconded, the chairman then restates the motion and by so doing puts the question to the meeting and opens the debate. When properly before the meeting a motion may be withdrawn by its mover and seconder *only* with the assent of the meeting as a whole. In the course of debate the motion may be amended in various ways, or action may be taken to delay or defer its effect, but it must remain before the meeting until it is finally disposed of in one way or another.

When a vote has been taken and the motion declared either carried or lost, that decision becomes formally the decision of the body in question and is so recorded. A question once decided cannot be brought up again at the same meeting, but if it should become necessary to rescind a motion that has been passed, notice of intention can be given at one meeting and a motion for rescinding be introduced and dealt with at a subsequent meeting. Ordinarily a motion that has once been negatived cannot be reintroduced; however, another motion of similar intent but differing in some particulars may be entertained at the discretion of the chairman.

The democratic right to introduce a proposition in the form of a motion, and of full debate and a free vote thereon, carries with it the obligation of the majority to respect its own decisions to the same extent as the obligation of a minority to accept and respect decisions of the majority. In other words, a decision reached by due process must be recognized and observed as such by all concerned; if it involves action, of whatever nature, that action must be taken.

37. Reconsideration

Notwithstanding the foregoing, procedures are sometimes provided for not only rescinding a motion decided in the affirmative, but also reconsidering a negative decision. A reconsideration rule usually provides that a person must give notice in writing that he will move at the next meeting that a question be reconsidered. The provision is a useful one, in that conclusions occasionally may be reached hastily or on the basis of inadequate information and a later review may well be in the general interest. It is nevertheless important that reconsideration not be allowed except upon due notice and formal motion, and it is customary to insist on a two-thirds majority vote on a motion to reconsider.

38. Amendments

If anyone qualified to debate a motion finds that, while acceptable in principle, it is deficient in any one or more of its terms, he may propose a motion to amend it. An amendment may change a word or words in a motion, may add words to it or delete words from it. It must not merely negate a motion, since this result can be obtained by voting against it. An amending motion may be introduced by stating "I move to amend the motion by substituting the words . . . with the words . . . so that the motion will read . . ." The amending motion must be seconded.

An amending motion must be strictly relevant to the main motion and be made while the main motion is under consideration. It must not alter in a material way the principle embodied in the main motion but should merely vary its terms in one or more particulars. The question of the propriety of a proposed amendment is one which the chairman must decide. Not infrequently a motion to amend will be introduced which is in reality a new motion, and the chairman should act promptly and firmly to rule it out of order.

Just as an amendment may be moved to a main motion, so an amendment may be moved to an amendment. The conditions applicable in the case of an original amendment are equally applicable to a secondary, or subamendment: it may propose a variation in the terms of the original amendment but it must not materially alter the underlying intent of either the original amendment or the main motion. Usually only two amendments to a question, namely an amendment and a subamendment, will be allowed at the same time. When one or both have been disposed of a further amendment or subamendment, as the case may be, may be entertained by the chair.

When there has been a main motion, an amendment and an

amendment in amendment, or subamendment, the procedure will be as follows:

Having satisfied himself that the subamendment has been fully discussed, the chairman puts the question "Shall the amendment in amendment (or subamendment) carry?" If it does, discussion continues on the amendment, as amended, at the conclusion of which the chairman puts the question "Shall the amendment as amended carry?"; or, if the subamendment was negatived his question is "Shall the amendment carry?" On an affirmative vote in either case discussion will continue on the main question as amended and the chairman's final question is "Shall the main motion as amended carry?"; or, if the amendment was defeated "Shall the main motion carry?"

It is to be noted that the procedure is always in reverse order, from subamendment through amendment to the main motion. An amendment may be introduced at any stage prior to the question being put on the main motion, provided there is not more than one amendment and one subamendment before the meeting at one time. If a member wishes to move an amendment, but it is not in order at the time in view of the fact that two amendments are already before the meeting, he may state his intention, as his proposal might affect the vote on those that are awaiting decision.

Provision for the introduction of amendments is an important procedural measure, but in the interests of clarity and despatch, undue complication is to be avoided if at all possible. This can sometimes be accomplished by forethought and consultation in the preparation of the main motion.

It is, again, the responsibility of the chairman to guide the meeting through the amending process to a clearly understood result carrying majority approval.

39. Notice of Motion

If a substantial issue is to be raised affecting the constitution, policies or procedures of a body, it is always advisable, and in some cases mandatory, that notice be given at one meeting that such issue will be introduced by motion at the next or a subsequent meeting. The notice is merely a statement of intention and may be made by any member at an appropriate time in the proceedings. It requires no seconder and is not at that time debatable.

The purpose of such notice is to permit the members of a body to consider and prepare for the question or questions that will be placed before them for consideration, thereby facilitating discussion and contributing to the efficient and satisfactory discharge of the matter. When an intention to introduce a motion has been announced, provision for the item should be made in the agenda of the meeting at which it is to be dealt with; the notice of this meeting should, moreover, refer to the item and if practicable should include the actual text of the motion to be introduced, with such explanatory material as may appear requisite.

In some organizations, constitutions or by-laws provide that notice be given of an intention to introduce certain classes of motions at a specific time or number of days before it can be considered.

Notice is not generally necessary in the case of amendments that are relevant to a motion, although it is to be noted that substantive questions may arise in connection with a motion of which special notice has been given. The raising of such new questions may necessitate, or at least make highly desirable, the giving of prior notice concerning them.

40. Motions for Special Purposes

In addition to a main motion, which offers a proposal, and amendments to vary the terms of a main motion, all debatable, there are certain motions which may be made while the debate is in progress and which for the most part are not themselves debatable or amendable. The principal class of motions in this category are called "dilatory" motions, since their effect is to supersede, delay or postpone the consideration of a question. They may be put in the course of debate but not so as to interrupt a speaker who has the floor.

The principal subsidiary motions are as follows:

(a) *Motion to Adjourn* – A motion to adjourn the debate or the meeting is always in order, must be seconded, but is not debatable. It is a means by which a decision on a question may be deferred. If the motion to adjourn carries, the matter under consideration must be put aside, but it can be re-instated at a later meeting. If it does not carry, the meeting proceeds as though no interruption had occurred.

(b) *Proceeding to Next Business* – A motion to proceed to the next business, or calling for the reading of the orders of the day, if carried, likewise sets aside the question then under consideration and the meeting proceeds to the next item on the agenda. If lost, discussion is resumed. The motion must be seconded, and must be put to the meeting forthwith without debate.

(c) *The Previous Question* – The motion known as "the previous question" is made in the form "I move that the question be now put." Its object is to prevent the proposing of amendments or any other intervening action and thus force a direct vote on the main question. The motion must be seconded and may be debated, but may not be amended. If resolved in the affirmative the question must be put forthwith on the main motion and a decision be reached which will dispose of it. A defeat of a motion for "the previous question" means in effect that the main motion may not be now put to the question, and it is thus superseded. The main motion may, however, be revived on a future day, as the negative of "the previous question" merely binds the Chair not to put the main question at that time.

Various usages have been applied at various times to "the previous question"; it should be employed with caution and with a clear understanding of the end it is intended to accomplish, *viz.*, a cessation of debate and no further action prior to a vote on the issue in question, or if the motion fails that such issue will be temporarily set aside.

(d) *Deferment* – Motions to postpone to a specified time, or indefinitely, or to table, are admissible, but are uncommon in Canadian practice. Questions properly before a meeting should be resolved one way or another, but if circumstances should arise to make it desirable to defer consideration of an issue for the time or indefinitely a motion may be so made; it must be seconded and it is debatable. If decided in the affirmative the motion to which it applies is removed from debate, with any amendments that may attach to it, and may not be re-introduced until either the time specified or until it is later revived on motion.

A motion to "lay on the table" is similar in effect, usually putting aside a question to attend to more urgent business. If a motion to table is carried, the main motion to which it is applied is laid aside, together with any amendments that may attach to it, but its consideration may be resumed at any time upon motion that the matter be taken from the table. The latter motion must be decided forthwith without amendment or debate.

(e) *Reference, or Committal* – If it should be decided that a subject demands fuller attention than can be given in a regular meeting a motion may be made that it be referred, or committed, to a standing or special committee. Such a motion may be amended and debated, but only with respect to the reference or committal, not the main subject at issue. It cannot be superseded by a motion to postpone or for "the previous question."

If a committee's eventual response on a matter referred to it is for any reason considered inadequate or unsatisfactory, the matter may be referred back (re-referred or recommitted) to the committee.

It is to be noted with respect to the above special motions that some, notably those to postpone and to table, are not drawn from Canadian parliamentary practice, and their employment should hence be countenanced only if there has been general prior agreement as to their acceptability, usage and effect. These and other rules of procedure have been developed in the United States, together with a whole system of usage and precedence. If it is felt desirable to adopt this system, such adoption should be clearly acknowledged, or special rules should be formed, so that those concerned should have no misapprehension of the conditions under which they are expected to function.

For the purposes of the great majority of meetings, where those attending cannot be expected to have a detailed acquaintance with all the possibilities of complex procedures, it usually will be found not only sufficient but actually advantageous to transact business under the simplest rules that meet the circumstances, based upon or adapted from those of the Canadian Parliament.

41. Debate

Meetings are held to permit those who qualify to express their views on the matters raised for consideration; every member possesses such a right provided he is prepared to exercise it within the agreed framework of rules and usages. In Parliament and many legislative or other public bodies there are rules which limit the number of times a member or participant may speak and the length of speeches, so that the total time available may be equitably shared. In less formal or smaller bodies and in committees such restrictions are not generally imposed, although the chairman may exercise discretion in this regard to prevent domination of the proceedings or an undue consumption of the time and patience of the assembly.

A member, having risen in his place or otherwise signified his desire to speak, should await recognition by the chairman. If two or more should so signify at the same time the chairman will call upon the one who first caught his attention and he may indicate at that time an order in which the other intending speakers may have the floor.

All remarks should be addressed to the chair. Even if a member who is speaking wishes to direct a question to some other member of the assembly, the question should properly be directed through the chair, as the chairman has the right to determine whether any matter is in order and to decline to permit a question to be put or any other action to be taken if in his opinion (subject to appeal) it would be contrary to the rules or acceptable usage or would offend propriety.

Remarks and arguments must be relevant to the question under consideration, and the chairman is the judge of relevancy. He is entitled to interrupt a speaker if he is deviating unduly from the main thread of the discussion. Otherwise a speaker has the right to be heard without interruption, unless he commits a breach of order or contravenes the rules under which the assembly functions. In such cases any member may interject and the speaker must cease and resume his seat until the matter has been dealt with.

Needless to say, remarks made in the course of a meeting should be in good taste, should not be capable of misinterpretation, and should give offence to no one.

The purposes of any meeting will be advanced by the observance of the proprieties in the course of debate. More latitude may be allowed in small and informal meetings, but in all cases it is imperative that the rights and sensibilities of all participants be observed.

42. Putting the Question
When a motion or an issue has been debated and it appears to the chairman that the meeting is prepared to dispose of it, he enquires

whether the meeting is ready for the question. Alternatively, he may halt proceedings at a specified time if it has been previously agreed to place any limit on debate.

If the chairman's enquiry whether the meeting is ready for the question meets with no objection, he will say "The question is as follows . . ." and proceeds to read the motion or describe the issue. He will call for those in favour to so signify, then those opposed. Even if it is apparent that those in favour predominate he should not fail to permit a negative expression, as there are frequently those who wish to make clear their opposition.

43. Methods of Voting

There are several ways in which a vote may be registered:

(a) *Voice* – The chairman may ask those in favour to say "aye" or "yea," then those opposed to say "nay," announcing that the ayes or the nays have it, as the case may be, and declaring the motion either carried or lost. This method, although commonly used in Parliament, possesses the disadvantage that when there is anything like an equal division of opinion the chairman is called upon to make a difficult decision as to which group of voices predominates. His opinion may be challenged and a motion introduced for a vote to be taken by another method. It is always undesirable to take a second vote on a single motion or issue, as some participants may be influenced by the first showing to change their vote for personal or expedient reasons, and a just accounting may hence not appear. Moreover, a difference in the outcome of a first and second vote may leave some participants with a suspicion of carelessness or even manipulation.

(b) *Show of Hands* – By far the commonest voting method in ordinary meetings is by a show of hands. Those for and those against the motion are, in turn, asked to raise their right hands; the hands are counted, the result announced, and the motion declared either carried or lost.

(c) *Standing Vote* – On certain issues it may be considered important to identify those in favour or opposed, and a motion may be introduced calling for a standing vote. If carried those supporting and those against the proposal under consideration are asked, separately, to stand, and they are counted. The method merely gives emphasis to the division of opinion and should be used with caution.

(d) *Ballot* – By-laws or regulations may require that votes on certain matters be registered by ballot, or a meeting itself may decide on motion that ballots be cast on a particular issue. In such an event, after the question has been put everyone qualified to vote is supplied with a ballot paper upon which he registers his vote; the completed ballots are collected and enumerated and the chairman announces the question decided in either the affirmative or negative. He need not announce the numerical count unless specifically required or requested to do so.

When a vote is to be taken by ballot it is proper, before balloting, to appoint scrutineers. They should be disinterested persons. Their duties are to ensure the proper conduct of the voting process, to count the completed ballots, and to give the result to the presiding officer.

(e) *Mail Ballot* – In large organizations where full attendance at a meeting is virtually impossible, provision may be incorporated in by-laws or regulations for a mail ballot on certain major issues, to give everyone who is qualified an opportunity to register an opinion. Firm rules should be drawn up to govern the conduct of such a procedure, and the appointment of scrutineers is again necessary.

Regardless of the voting procedure employed, it must be and it must be seen to be carried out with absolute fairness to an unequivocal result.

On important issues regulations often provide that there must be a two-thirds majority for a motion to carry: in routine business a simple majority is sufficient. On an equality of votes the motion is lost. Unless otherwise provided the chairman has the same voting rights as other members, and he is usually accorded a second or casting vote when the votes for and against have been equal.

When routine items are being dealt with, or it is obvious that there is no objection to a proposal under discussion, the chairman may dispense with a formal vote and merely say "If there is no objection . . ." and assume general assent. If someone objects a vote must be taken.

44. Order

For the purposes of formal assemblies the word "order" has more than one connotation. The chairman calls the meeting to order when he wants to quiet extraneous activity and channel attention to the business at hand. There is an order of procedure for an organized body laid down in its by-laws or other regulatory material. Order also means decorum and plain good behaviour. It is the chairman's duty to see that order in all senses is observed and preserved.

If in the course of debate a member says or does anything that is contrary to the rules or established custom he should be immediately called to order by the chairman and should not be allowed to continue an irregular or offensive procedure. A simple admonition: "Order, please," is usually sufficient to correct a minor departure from acceptable usage, but if the offense is material to the proper conduct of the proceedings the chairman may need to say: "Mr. ____, you are out of order," in which event the speaker should take his seat while the chairman explains the point. The chairman's ruling is not debatable and it is usually accepted. It may be challenged, however, on a duly seconded motion to dissent from the ruling of the chair. If such a motion receives majority support the chairman's ruling is overturned.

Any member may at any time rise on a point of order, interrupting a speaker if necessary, to point out a breach of rules. As before the speaker should resume his seat while the point is cleared, and it becomes the chairman's duty to rule whether the point is well taken and to direct accordingly.

The maintenance of order, meaning the absence of interference with calm deliberation and the preservation of conditions permitting the effective conduct of the assembly's affairs, is a responsibility of the presiding officer, and one which he must be at all times ready and able to discharge. If there is disturbance he should courteously halt the meeting, interrupting a speaker if he must, call for order, and if necessary admonish the offenders. Should conditions develop which make it appear that order cannot be restored by simple admonition, the chairman may recess the meeting for a brief period, leaving the chair, or, in the event of a serious disturbance, he may adjourn the meeting to another day.

In normal circumstances difficulties of this kind rarely occur, but they are by no means unknown and anyone undertaking the duties of presiding officer should be prepared to exercise the qualities of discretion and firmness necessary to deal with them.

It is to be noted that a presiding officer usually does not himself possess the right to discipline an offending member or impose penalties. Should such a course seem necessary, it should be taken only on the basis of a proposal offered on motion and bearing the approval of a substantial majority of the whole body. However, if a meeting of an organized body is designed for the attendance only of members of that body and there are non-members present, the chairman may, if circumstances warrant, request the withdrawal of such non-members and may take such measures as may be necessary to enforce his request.

Slander is oral and libel written defamation of the character of another. Both are actionable in law and every participant in an assembly should be alert to the possible consequences of intemperate or injurious statements.

45. Privilege

Questions of privilege may be raised in the course of debate, but not so as to interrupt a speaker who has the floor. Such questions usually have to do with the rights or interests of the assembly as a whole or of a member personally and arise if in the course of debate it appears that those rights or interests are adversely affected. The chairman must decide if the question is properly one of privilege and admissible (subject to appeal) and if he decides in the affirmative the matter must be dealt with forthwith and be disposed of before debate on the main issue is resumed.

In another sense the term privileged is applied to remarks made in a closed meeting which if made publicly might be considered actionable. Statements made in Parliament, for example, are considered to be privileged even though in ordinary circumstances they might be regarded as defamatory. In ordinary assemblies it would be unwise to assume privilege, as an ultimate decision would rest with the courts if action were taken.

46. Closing the Meeting

When all the purposes for which a meeting has been convoked have been fulfilled, and the chairman is satisfied that there is no other business that can properly be dealt with, he simply announces that the meeting is closed or terminated. He needs no motion or other authority for so doing.

There are, however, other circumstances under which a meeting may be ended:

(a) If orders or regulations provide that meetings conclude by a specified time, the chairman must halt the meeting at that time whether or not all of its purposes have been accomplished, items remaining on the agenda being carried forward to the next or a subsequent meeting, *unless* a motion is adopted abrogating the rule for the purposes of that particular meeting. If in the course of a meeting a resolution is adopted that the meeting conclude not later than a specified hour, the chairman must carry out the instruction.

(b) A motion to adjourn is always in order and if adopted it must be given effect regardless of the stage of the proceedings.

(c) If circumstances should develop, e.g., a need to secure information, the chairman may recess the meeting, or he may *suggest* that it adjourn to another day. In the latter event his suggestion must receive majority concurrence in the form of an appropriate motion duly seconded and carried.

(d) Should a meeting become disorderly beyond the control of the chairman, he may, on his own initiative, either recess it or adjourn it to another day.

(e) In the absence of a quorum at the commencement of a meeting or at any time in its progress, the meeting is or becomes automatically improperly constituted and the chairman normally has no alternative but to adjourn it to another day.

47. Minutes and Records
Minutes are a record of proceedings and they are an integral part of the operation of any organized body. The responsibility for preparing and maintaining the minutes falls upon the secretary, recording secretary, clerk or other officer specifically appointed for the purpose. He should take notes while the meeting is in progress and prepare a typewritten or fair copy of the complete minutes as soon as possible thereafter. Copies of all minutes should be kept in a consecutive order in a binder, and in this form they become an important record of an organization's proceedings and a point of reference with respect to its decisions.

The minutes of each meeting should record the place, date and time at which it was held; the name of the presiding officer; either a list of those attending or other evidence of the presence of a quorum, and any other detail that might be considered relevant, such as the attendance of guests.

The minutes should accurately record the items of business placed before the meeting and the actions taken and decisions reached concerning them. They should not attempt a verbatim account of the debate, but may include references to major points adduced in the course of debate. Generally speaking the names of those who engage in discussion are not specified, but names may be used if they appear to be directly relevant to the issue under consideration. The primary aim in the preparation of minutes should be to combine completeness and clarity with succinctness.

The first order of business at most meetings will be the reading and approval, or confirmation, of the minutes of the immediately preceding meeting. If, after reading, an error is detected, the necessary correction should be made at once and the minutes may then be approved as corrected. It is improper to raise a discussion on the policy or merits of a question dealt with in the minutes, and in the event of attention being directed to an alleged error remarks at this point should relate strictly to the matter of the error.

Procedures at a meeting can be facilitated by distributing copies of minutes to those entitled to receive them in advance of the meeting at which they would normally be read. Distribution in advance serves a double purpose in that it reminds those who were in attendance, and informs those who were not, of the business transacted; it also abbreviates the time required for dealing with minutes, since they may be taken as read and confirmed by a simple motion.

When the minutes have been approved the copy of record may be signed by the presiding officer, although his endorsement has only a legal significance.

Other papers pertaining to an organization's transactions such as reports, financial statements, etc., must also be preserved by the secretary and/or treasurer, or by such other official as may be designated. Customarily these records are considered as being available for inspection for legitimate purposes by any member of the organization in good standing, but for practical purposes it is best to provide that a request to inspect be channelled through a senior officer.

Reports or other documents comprising an important element in the business of a meeting may be appended to the minutes of that meeting and by reference be made an integral part thereof.

48. Committees

Committees are an important means whereby a subject may receive more detailed and effective consideration than is possible at a full and formal meeting, or when considerable time, investigation or consultation may be involved.

A committee of the whole is a device regularly used by legislative bodies to permit freer debate and detailed examination of bills, reports, and the like. It is created by a motion that the body resolve itself into a committee of the whole, whereupon the presiding officer resigns the Chair to a chairman appointed for the purpose. Upon the completion of its function the presiding officer resumes the chair, the committee of the whole reports its findings, and formal action is taken upon the findings by the body in its official capacity. There is little need for employment of this device in the conduct of the affairs of private organizations.

Standing committees are appointed in order to have available a cohesive body to which may be referred questions which may arise from time to time in defined areas of an organization's interests, or to which may be assigned a continuing responsibility in those areas. They may be, for example, committees on finance, on membership, on program, or the like, their personnels being revised annually or from time to time as requisite.

Special committees may be appointed at any time it is desired to refer an issue for special consideration, and they exist for only as long as may be necessary to discharge that function. Special committees are appointed usually in a proposal originating in the whole assembly, the naming of the individuals to comprise a committee, including a chairman, being the prerogative of the presiding officer, with or without suggestions from others.

Committees may arrange their own procedures, provided they do not contravene any of the directives they may have received from, or the general regulations governing, the main body. A committee may, however, deal only with such matters as have been referred to it by the body that appoints it; it is not at liberty to go beyond its terms of reference. Its eventual report must, moreover, be made to the appointive body and to no other; it is improper for any committee decision or finding to be conveyed to outside interests prior to its report being made to the originating body, and indeed even after its report has been made it should not feel itself free to disseminate information concerning it unless specifically authorized to do so. A commitee is, in other words, strictly a creature of the body that created it.

When a special committee's duties have been fully discharged it may consider itself dissolved; if it reaches an impasse and cannot achieve its objective it may request dissolution.

A committee may consist of any number of individuals, even one. The work of most committees will be facilitated if their number is small and their members are chosen for their qualification to deal with the subject at issue.

A sub-committee is a division of a committee appointed to deal with an aspect of the latter's concerns; again, it is responsible to and reports to the body appointing it.

An executive committee usually possesses somewhat specialized characteristics, being constituted of individuals, commonly the officers of the organization, as specified in by-laws or regulations. It may possess fairly wide policy-making and administrative powers, but it should nevertheless always recognize its responsibility to the parent body.

Unless otherwise stipulated, a quorum at a meeting of a committee is a majority of its members.

49. Reports

The report of a committee to its appointive body should contain all of the information requisite for action thereon.

When a report is made by a committee of the whole incorporating recommendations, a motion for its adoption and hence concurrence in the recommendations, should be put forthwith and be decided without debate or amendment.

A report emanating from a standing committee is sometimes of a routine nature and may be received merely for information. If it contains recommendations it becomes subject to debate and amendment.

The report of a special committee should deal exclusively with the item or items that have been referred for the committee's consideration, commencing with a statement of those items and proceeding to a specific recommendation concerning them. The latter may be a proposal in the form of a motion. Such a report is subject to debate and amendment.

If a committee's work extends over a long period a progress report may be made, either orally or in writing; in this case no action is required, but the main body receiving the report may give its committee further advice or directives. A committee's final report is preferably in writing and furnished in advance of the meeting at which it is to be considered. The practice of supplying a sufficient number of copies of a report to permit distribution in advance of such meeting to those expected to attend permits prior consideration and will save time at the meeting.

Reports should be clear and concise. They need not set out in detail the considerations leading to a conclusion or proposal, unless these are cogent and directly relevant to the issue and its determination. A report should be signed by the chairman of the committee producing it, and if it is desired to give particular emphasis it may be signed by all members of the committee. Its presentation is usually made by the chairman of the committee.

A report may be merely received, which signifies that it has been accepted and duly noted but that no pursuant action is contemplated. This course is taken if the report is essentially informative, or it may represent a decision against proceeding with a proposal contained therein for the time being. In such a case receipt of the report is recorded and its proposals may be revived at a later date.

Reports, other than those of a committee of the whole, are subject to debate and amendment. The body that has appointed the committee and received its report may alter or adjust the terms of any proposal or may decline to accept the proposal. If it is felt that a report fails in ways that cannot be conveniently corrected by immediate amendment, the report may be referred back to the committee for further study and revision.

The adoption of a report implies the obligation to give effect to all of its recommendations, either in their original form or as amended.

It is obvious that a committee's report should bear the support of at least a majority of the committee's members. If there are irreconcilable differences within the committee, the dissidents may issue a minority report as a means of recording their opposite views. A minority report is not acted upon, however, unless it is submitted with a motion that it be adopted in substitution for the majority report.

50. General

The degree of formality to be observed in the conduct of a meeting depends upon whether or not a system of procedures is laid down in a constitution or in by-laws and regulations, and, if it is not so laid down, upon custom and usage developed by general agreement over a period of time. Even in the absence of any formal directive it is of the utmost importance that the basic rules of order be understood and observed; otherwise participants are made unsure of their rights and limitations, controls are weakened, and the authenticity of decisions may be open to question. Slovenly, indifferent and confused procedure is antagonistic to good will and the successful prosecution of business.

Nevertheless, a fussy dependence upon procedural minutiae can be equally frustrating and non-productive. Insistence upon a rigmarole of rules possessing limited applicability and with which many participants may be unfamiliar can be time-consuming and might well hamper the easy flow of meaningful discussion.

The objective should be a well understood system sufficient for but not exceeding the needs of a particular set of circumstances.

Small groups often function best in an informal atmosphere, and even in a formal meeting conditions may arise making it desirable to open a subject for informal discussion. The chairman, however, should never lose control of even these proceedings, and at their conclusion he should be certain that any decisions reached are properly based and duly recorded.

Should doubt arise with respect to any rules of procedure, reference may be had to the orders applicable in the Canadian House of Commons, so far as they may be applicable.

PART III

ASSEMBLIES AND ORGANIZATIONS

51. Lawful and Unlawful Assemblies

By Section 1 of the Canadian Bill of Rights it is recognized and declared that " . . . in Canada there have existed and shall continue to exist without discrimination by reason of race, national origin, colour, religion or sex, the following human rights and fundamental freedoms, namely freedom of speech, and freedom of assembly and association."

This is a statement of principle conferring a right of public meeting, but it does not exempt any group of persons, occupying a public place so as to interfere with the ordinary rights of citizens under the law, from the charge of creating a nuisance or committing a trespass. A number of persons may assemble for any lawful purpose, and provided they do not infringe any law they should be subject to no interference by other persons who may not approve of the object of the meeting.

The conduct of a meeting may in itself call into question its legality. By Canadian criminal law:

An unlawful assembly is an assembly of three or more persons who, with intent to carry out any common purpose, assemble in such a manner or so conduct themselves when they are assembled as to cause persons in the neighbourhood of the assembly to fear, on reasonable grounds, that they (a) will disturb the peace tumultuously, or (b) will by that assembly needlessly and without reasonable cause provoke other persons to disturb the peace tumultuously.

A lawful assembly may thus become an unlawful one if by its conduct it creates conditions which, had they existed at the outset, would have made the assembly unlawful at the outset.

52. Procedure at Public Meetings

When a number of persons assemble at an appointed place and time in response to a public notice or advertisement for the purpose of discussing a matter of public interest, it is incumbent upon someone who may be responsible for convoking the meeting, or who may be otherwise directly concerned with its purposes, to call it to order and to request the nomination of a chairman. A motion "That Mr. ____ do take the Chair" should be seconded and be formally put to the meeting. Should more than one person be nominated – an infrequent occurrence – each name is dealt with in the order of nomination, the same person continuing to act as temporary director of the proceedings until a chairman is elected.

The chairman so chosen, having established order, requests the meeting to appoint a secretary to keep a record of the proceedings. When a secretary has been chosen in the same manner as the chairman, he immediately assumes his duties, carefully noting any decisions reached.

A meeting is ordinarily able to proceed with the business for which it was called only after it has been regularly constituted by the election of a chairman and secretary.

To begin, the chairman should read the notice or advertisement calling the meeting, if any, or in the absence of such notice inform the meeting briefly of its object, and he should then call upon such persons as he knows are especially interested to address the assembly. The chairman may at his discretion limit the length of speeches and the number of times an individual may participate in the discussion, but he should make clear that he does so to conserve time and to permit the widest possible expression of opinion.

If a meeting is held for a specific purpose – to express an opinion on a question of the day or to promote some charitable, benevolent or other public project – those responsible should be ready with motions or propositions which will assist the assembly to come to a conclusion on the matter under discussion. However, care should be exercised to avoid creating the impression that certain individuals are endeavouring to influence the proceedings unduly.

The rules to be followed in the conduct of a public meeting are those applicable in any meeting. Motions and amendments must be properly put and debated and decisions must be reached by due process. The chairman should remain impartial and take no active part in the debate. As in every type of meeting he should display firmness, courtesy and tact, and be willing, within the limits of the time available, to allow – indeed, encourage – a full expression of opinion. Should the assembly become unruly, or the speakers act or speak improperly, the chairman should interpose and make such appeals for good conduct as his judgement will dictate. If the meeting gets beyond his control he may declare the assembly at an end and leave the Chair; by so doing he destroys the meeting's constitutionality and it has no right to carry on.

When a subject has, in the opinion of the Chair, been fully discussed, and it appears that the meeting is ready to vote, the chairman asks: "Is the meeting ready for the question?" On affirmative evidence he then requests those in favour of the motion or the proposal to so indicate by raising their right hand, and similarly with those opposed. The votes are counted by the secretary, or sometimes by tellers who have been appointed for the purpose in advance, and the tally being announced the chairman declares the motion carried or lost as the case may be. The secretary and the tellers, if any, are entitled to add their votes to those of the assembly. In the case of an equality of votes the motion is lost, but in such a case the chairman may then cast his vote; he should however be aware of the effect of such action and he may wish to explain the reason for his vote. If someone votes in error he should so declare and have the error rectified before the chairman announces the final decision on the question; otherwise the vote cannot be changed. It is important that proper steps be taken to ensure that the voting procedure leads to a clear-cut result and thus avoid a demand that the vote be taken again.

A voice vote (calling for "yeas" and "nays") is usually not practicable in a public assembly, nor is one requiring those present to rise in their places to be counted. As a rule a ballot is impracticable at public meetings and should be used only in exceptional circumstances in which it may be considered essential to preserve the secrecy of the individual votes.

When the business of a meeting has been concluded, the chairman asks: "Is there any other matter before the meeting?" He may use discretion as to the admissibility of other items of business, on the grounds of their relevancy. If a meeting has been called for a specific purpose he should have no hesitation in declining to admit clearly extraneous matters for discussion. If there is no further business the chairman formally declares the meeting closed and leaves the Chair.

53. Formation of Associations, Societies, etc.

Should it be proposed to establish an association for any legitimate purpose, as for example the forwarding of common business interests or scholarly studies, or the pursuit of benevolent, recreational or other objects, the promoters of such a project should first consult among themselves to assure themselves of its practicability. Having done so, and agreed upon a general outline, notice should be given, by advertisement or otherwise, announcing the time and place of a meeting for organizational purposes.

The interested persons being assembled, one of the promoters calls the meeting to order and suggests the election of temporary officers (a chairman and secretary) for the purposes of the meeting. They are elected by the same procedure employed for ordinary public assemblies (see preceding article).

The chairman reads the notice calling the meeting; he may add brief remarks that he considers cogent, and he then calls for comment from those in attendance. The meeting should be conducted informally to encourage free and full debate, and no rules need be laid down. Good sense and relevancy are the desirable qualities on the part of the speakers; tact and judgement are, as usual, the requisites of the chair. Although there may be some preliminary discussion of a general nature, at some early point in the proceedings someone should propose, and another second, a formal motion as a basis of a debate leading to a conclusion. Such a motion might be: "That in the opinion of this meeting it is desirable to form a society to encourage studies in current literature (or whatever the special object might be)."

After a full discussion the motion should be put by the Chair. If it carries, action should be taken to give substance to the decision. Someone might move: "That a committee of (number) be appointed, comprising Messrs (names), to frame a constitution for a society to encourage studies in current literature and to report thereon at a meeting to be called at (place, date and hour)." The name, nature and function of the proposed society may then be left for recommendation by the committee so appointed, or the chairman may allow further brief discussion as a guide to the committee. If a name for the society has been suggested, or is considered of special importance, it may be put forward in a motion and dealt with at the preliminary meeting.

The preliminary meeting then adjourns until the day and hour appointed, when it resumes with the same chairman and secretary. If they are absent, two others are appointed in their place. The chairman calls for the reading and approval of the minutes of the last meeting, then enquires whether the committee appointed to frame a constitution is ready to report. If it is, the report is read, usually by the committee chairman. It should be a written majority report, bearing the signature of the chairman of the committee. It should begin by stating the order of reference, as follows: "The committee appointed to frame a constitution for a society to encourage studies in modern literature (or whatever the purpose may be) respectfully submits the following as a recommendation": then follows the draft of the constitution. The chairman of the committee then moves "That the report be now considered," and when his motion is seconded, put to the meeting and agreed to, the document is open to debate, amendment and adoption.

The report should be considered in detail, that is paragraph by paragraph, each being subject to discussion, approval or amendment.

When a constitution has been adopted, the chairman may call upon the persons present who wish to become members to sign a roll or membership prepared by the secretary. These are the charter members. A recess may be called for this purpose.

On resuming, the acting chairman will take the sense of the meeting – strictly speaking, of the members of the new society as they appear on the roll duly signed – whether to proceed at once with the election of officers. If agreed, nominations are requested for each of the offices designated in the constitution, usually a president, one or more vice-presidents, a secretary, a treasurer, and sometimes a council. Each nomination is voted on, and in the event of more than one nomination being made for a single office a vote is taken on each name in the order of nomination. On these occasions a show of hands is all that is required. Balloting is rarely necessary and should be employed only if a formal motion to that effect has been passed before the meeting proceeds to the election of officers.

When the officers have been duly elected the temporary chairman and secretary vacate their places, assuming that they have not themselves been elected to these offices, and the new officers assume their duties.

It is in order then for a motion to be made to appoint a committee – a small committee is preferable – to draft by-laws, a code of rules of procedure or such other regulatory material as may be considered necessary and not embodied in the constitution itself. The committee that framed the constitution is often re-appointed for this additional duty, and indeed it is not unusual for such a committee to be given the authority to draft both a constitution and regulations in the first instance. It should be noted, however, that the two serve different purposes: a constitution states the basic principles underlying an organization's existence; by-laws or other regulatory material are designed to provide for internal management. The latter are best left to be compiled after the steps necessary for formal organization have been completed.

Having appointed a committee to prepare the rules, a meeting should adjourn to permit the committee to function. It may first deal with any urgent items, but not such as may evoke controversy; rules of procedure should be decided before the organization launches its program of activities.

Procedure at the meeting convoked for the purpose of receiving and considering the report of the committee appointed to draft the regulations is similar in all respect to that observed at the meeting to deal with the constitution. The various proposed items are discussed in order and approved, disapproved or amended. When all have been considered, it is customary for a motion to be made and seconded that the report as presented or as amended be adopted, and if the motion carries the regulations as drafted thereupon become the regulations of the organization until such time as they may be further amended by due process. If the committee's report is substantially unacceptable it may be referred back to the committee for further study and revision, preferably with a statement of its inadequacies.

It is of immeasurable assistance to have reports embodying the draft of a constitution or by-laws or other regulations prepared in sufficient number that they may be distributed to those concerned in advance of any meeting at which they are to be considered. Their proper examination is thereby facilitated and action at the meeting made more effective.

As there are no agreed rules in effect at the meetings at which the constitution and regulations are under consideration, there should be an understanding that rules commonly observed will apply, but the chairman may at his discretion invoke such limitations upon debate as may be considered necessary, or otherwise act to ensure equitable and efficient procedures.

54. Draft Constitution

An organization's constitution is the basis of its existence, its fundamental law. In it are set out its name, object, the designation of its principal officers, the nature of and qualification for membership, and such conditions, limitations or other considerations as may be necessary to establish the body's essential character. The preparation of such a document may require expert advice, but for the many relatively small organizations that nevertheless need a proper constitutional basis there follows a typical form of constitution. Needless to say, it may be modified and adapted to individual needs.

The purposes and objects of the association shall be the encouragement and promotion of studies in modern literature. Any profits or other accretions to the association shall be used in the promotion of the aforementioned objects.

The membership of the association shall consist of two classes, namely: (1) active, and (2) honorary.

Active membership shall be open to any resident of this community upon payment of a membership fee in an amount to be determined from time to time at general meetings of the association.

Honorary members shall be elected from among persons in this community who are well known for their interests and activities in the promotion of studies in modern literature.

The officers of the association shall be the following: president, first vice-president, second vice-president, secretary and treasurer.

The officers shall be elected at annual meetings of the association to serve for a period of one year.

The officers shall serve as a management committee of the association, of which three shall be a quorum. The management committee may meet from time to time but not less frequently than once in every calendar month.

Notices of annual and general meetings of the association shall be directed by mail to each member of record, and/or may be given by advertisement in a local newspaper, not less than four days prior to the date of any such meeting, and shall state the place, date, time and purpose thereof.

The annual meeting of the association shall be held in April of each year upon a date fixed by the management committee. General meetings may be called from time to time as determined by the management committee.

The business to be transacted at annual meetings shall be: consideration and adoption of the minutes of the immediately preceding annual meeting; consideration of reports of the treasurer and president; the election of officers; the appointment of auditors; any other business that the management committee decides may properly come before the annual meeting.

The presence of not less than twenty members in good standing shall be necessary to constitute a quorum at any general meeting of the association.

A general meeting of the association shall be held within seven days after the filing with the secretary of a requisition to that effect in writing, signed by not less than twenty members in good standing of the association.

The president shall preside at all meetings of the association and of its management committee. In his absence, the duties of his office shall be performed by the senior vice-president then present.

Unless otherwise provided, questions arising at any meeting shall be decided by a majority vote of those present. When the votes are equal, but not otherwise, the chairman shall have a vote.

If any office becomes vacant, the management committee may elect any member in good standing to that office for the unexpired term.

The secretary shall keep a record in minutes of the proceedings of the meetings of the association and the management committee. The secretary shall have custody of all books, records and papers of the association, except such as shall be in the custody of the treasurer or other person authorized to have possession of them by resolution of the association.

The treasurer shall have supervision of all of the moneys and securities belonging to the association and shall cause all moneys received to be deposited in a chartered bank to be designated by the management committee. Such moneys shall be drawn out by cheques signed by the president and the treasurer, but in the absence of either or both of these officers, either of the vice-presidents may act on behalf of the absent officer or officers.

The financial year of the association shall end on the 31st day of March of each year.

The books of the association shall be audited prior to the annual meeting each year by a person or persons as appointed from time to time.

The association may devise and give effect to such by-laws, rules or regulations as may be requisite for its governance, provided they are consonant with the principles embodied in this constitution.

The constitution of the association may be amended at annual meetings, provided that a notice of motion to so amend has been filed with the secretary not less than ten days prior to such annual meeting. An amendment of the constitution shall be effected only with the support of two-thirds of the members voting at the annual meeting.

----

55. Election of Officers

Associations should prescribe in their by-laws or other regulatory material the procedures to be followed in the election of their officers. The outcome is important and the method should be fully understood and meticulously observed.

The usual first step is the appointment of a nominating committee, whose duty is to ensure that there is a nominee for each elective office. A nominating committee may be appointed by an executive or management committee, or by a general meeting on the latter's recommendation. It should be relatively small, and consist of individuals having a knowledge of the association's affairs, carrying general respect and being free of prejudice.

In the execution of its duties the nominating committee should give consideration to the qualities of the individuals eligible for election, and may take into account such things as diversities of interest, specific capabilities for performing particular functions, territorial representation in the case of an organization operating over a wide territory, and the like. Before making a nomination the committee must ensure that the proposed nominee is prepared to act if elected. It is not improper to nominate a member of the nominating committee, although such a member may then feel obliged to withdraw from the committee. Nor is it improper for the nominating committee to nominate more than one individual for a single office, knowing that such action will precipitate an election for that office.

Having completed its slate of nominees, the nominating committee reports its recommendations to the annual meeting or such other meeting as may be called for the election of officers.

In some organizations there is provision that nominations may also be made by any member in writing, bearing the assent of the nominee, provided such nominations are received by a stipulated date in advance of the meeting at which elections are to be held. As well, it is frequently provided that nominations may be made from the floor at the election meeting, but in such circumstances care must be taken to ensure that the nominee is present to signify his willingness to act if elected, or that his consent has been obtained beforehand. Written nominations or those from the floor are sometimes required to be supported by two or more members as nominators.

When the report of a nominating committee is adopted without question and without additional nominations being made, and if it contains only one nominee for each elective office, those nominated are at once declared duly elected by acclamation. A motion "That nominations be closed" has, if carried, the same effect.

If there are a number of offices to be filled, the chairman of the meeting at which the nominating committee's report is being considered may deal with each nomination separately. The nominee for each office being announced, the chairman will ask: "Are there any other nominations?" and allow sufficient time for such other nominations to be made. In each case any member may move that nominations be closed. If no such motion is made and there are no further nominations the chairman may say: "There being no further nominations, the nomination for — is closed and Mr. — is duly elected by acclamation."

In such cases of the election of a nominee by acclamation, the presiding officer may request the secretary to cast a single ballot for the nominee, but this procedure is not essential.

Some organizations provide for a meeting being held for the exclusive purpose of receiving nominations. The report of the nominating committee is then submitted at such a meeting and is acted upon as described above, with opportunity being given for additional nominations to be made from the floor. If the nominating committee's report is adopted *in toto,* or if no additional nominations are made, the committee's nominees are declared elected by acclamation and no further election procedures are necessary. Should there be further nominations made at a nomination meeting, so that there are more than one nominee for any elective office, arrangements must be made for the conduct of an election for such office or offices. The election should not be held at a meeting called for the sole purpose of receiving nominations.

An election, if required, should be conducted in full conformity with any and all conditions laid down in by-laws or regulations.

It is always desirable for elections to be decided by votes cast by ballot, as this provides absolute freedom of choice and secrecy, and avoids the possibility of personality conflict. Ballots should be prepared in advance, and they should contain only such information as is necessary to identify each nominee, with space for the marking of an X opposite each name. A few fair and impartial persons should be appointed as scrutineers of the ballots, or tellers, their responsibility being to decide the acceptability of the ballots cast, rejecting those improperly marked, to tally the votes, and to deliver a signed and sealed report of the result of the balloting to the secretary or such other official as may be designated to receive it.

Care should be taken to ensure that ballots are distributed only to those entitled to receive them, and that the official ballots are readily identifiable. All members in good standing of an organization, including its officers, are normally qualified to vote in elections.

Some organizations, particularly those operating over a wide territory, may find their purposes best served by the distribution and return of ballots by mail. The procedure is quite proper, but arrangements must be made for the returned, marked ballots to be received unopened by the scrutineers and retained wholly in their control.

Elections are usually decided by plurality, that is, the one receiving the largest number of votes by whatever margin wins. The regulations of some bodies require that election be by a majority vote, in which case to win a candidate must have not less than one more than half the total number of votes cast. In the case of a tie vote, the tie being substantiated by recount, another election should properly be held, with the contestants the two candidates whose votes were equal. Other tie-breaking procedures may be employed by common consent.

Sometimes, when a candidate has been elected by a majority vote, it will be moved that the vote supporting him be declared unanimous. The intent is to place on record that his election is totally supported, even though there were initially votes opposing him. There is no obligation to support such a motion, but it is bad form to debate it.

The presiding officer at a meeting at which elections were conducted, or at which the results of an election were announced, continues to occupy the Chair until all the business of that meeting has been dealt with. At the conclusion of that meeting he will install the newly-elected officer with appropriate remarks, and the latter, having assumed the Chair and made such remarks as he deems suitable, then immediately closes the meeting. This procedure is of course effective only if the by-laws or regulations do not provide that those elected assume office at some future, specified time.

56. Incorporation

Most bodies organized for social, scholarly, charitable or similar purposes function adequately under constitutions and by-laws of their own devising. However, an organization that grows to significant size either in terms of membership or territorial extent, or develops characteristics involving financial responsibilities, property ownership, public exposure etc., may find it necessary or desirable to acquire a legal existence as a means of being competent to transact its affairs with, and of being protected by, statutory authority.

Such bodies may be incorporated by a special act of either the federal or provincial parliaments of Canada, or in some cases under prevailing omnibus acts. More commonly their incorporation will be under letters patent, and there are special provisions in both the federal and provincial Companies Acts for the incorporation of organizations of a non-profit nature formed to carry on social, philanthropic, scientific, professional and similar operations.

There are formal procedures to be observed in making application for incorporation, and any organization contemplating this step should secure legal advice, and employ legal services if it is decided to proceed.

57. Winding Up

Should an association or society decide for any reason to wind up its affairs and bring its organized existence to an end, a regular procedure should be followed. The decision may stem from a lack of interest, an inability to attain objectives, an insufficiency of funds, or even extreme personality conflict, but whatever the cause, notice should be given at a general meeting that at the next or a subsequent general meeting a motion will be introduced that the organization be wound up and its effective existence terminated as of a specified date or a date to be fixed. When such a motion is introduced and seconded it is open to debate, in the course of which arguments for and against the proposed winding up should be fully aired. The members should be informed from the Chair that, to pass, the motion will require the support of not less than two-thirds of those present and qualified to vote.

At the same meeting it is desirable that authority be given, on motion, to the management or executive committee, or to a special committee appointed for the purpose, to give effect to the winding up resolution. This will entail the disposition of whatever assets the organization may possess in the form either of properties, physical goods (books, records, furnishings, etc.) or of monies. Provision should be made for the safekeeping of records, and it is in particular essential that an acceptable procedure be found for the disposition of whatever funds may remain in the treasury. Such funds belong in reality to the members and the method of their disposal is hence subject to their approval.

Should complications arise in the winding up process it is advisable to seek disinterested accounting and/or legal advice and assistance. The winding up of an incorporated body involves compliance with statutory procedures and legal services are indispensable.

58. Meetings for Special Purposes
Some types of meetings fall into a rather special category.

The major political parties, for example, have constitutions and codes of procedure governing the holding of conventions and meetings for the purpose of electing party leaders and nominating candidates for public office, or for framing party programs at the national or provincial levels. The principles of parliamentary law regulate order and decorum on all such occasions, but the machinery employed by units of these organizations, while conforming with an overall pattern, may differ from time to time and place to place. Frequently a special committee will be set up to organize these events, devise a program, and provide a procedural outline for the guidance of the officer who will preside.

An illustration, in general terms, would be a meeting of a local political organization convoked to nominate a candidate for election to the provincial or federal parliament. The executive of the local association will first meet to decide a closing date for the receipt of nominations, the place and date of a nominating meeting, and such other arrangements as may need to be made. Usually notice will be given, by advertisement or otherwise, that nominations must be filed not later than a specific date, some time ahead of the date of the meeting, specifying the place, date and time of the meeting, and making it clear that only members in good standing of the association (paid-up by a certain date) will be eligible to vote.

The meeting being convened, after proper notice, the president of the association customarily takes the Chair. Routine business is disposed of and the chairman introduces the main business of nominations. The constitution of the association may specify the nomination procedures, but if they do not the procedures should be agreed upon. It should, for instance, be understood that voting will be by ballot and whether a plurality or majority vote is required; whether limitations will be imposed on the length and number of speeches; that parliamentary rules will apply in debate, etc. Scrutineers, or tellers, of the ballot should be appointed.

If nominations from the floor are acceptable, any member may rise and propose a name, with such brief remarks as he deems appropriate. His motion being seconded, the chairman enquires whether there are other nominations. Should there be only one nomination, any rule requiring a ballot is ordinarily suspended and the chairman declares the nominee to be the unanimous choice of the meeting.

When there are several nominations for a single office, made either in writing previous to the meeting or from the floor, an election must be held. Occasionally a nominee, at some stage in the proceedings, will decline the nomination, but this is not a desirable occurrence; good practice dictates that the name of a person should not be put forward unless he has indicated his willingness to stand for election beforehand.

The candidates are usually accorded the privilege of addressing the meeting briefly. Then ballots are distributed by the tellers to those entitled to vote, are collected and counted by the tellers when they have been marked, and the result is reported to the presiding officer, who announces it to the meeting.

If, as is common in meetings of this kind, a candidate must obtain a majority of the total votes cast, to win, and if in the first ballot no candidate obtained such a majority, the name of the candidate receiving the smallest number of votes on the first ballot is dropped and another ballot is taken on those remaining. The process is repeated until a candidate is elected by an absolute majority of the votes cast.

Another method of balloting is for the secretary or clerk to call the roll of the members or delegates alphabetically, and as each comes forward they are given a ballot which they at once mark and return to the secretary for deposit in a box. When all have voted the ballots are counted by the scrutineers and the result announced in the usual way. While more time-consuming, the procedure has the merit of recording each voter, avoiding any possibility of error in the distribution and collection of ballots, and ensuring secrecy.

It may not be inappropriate here to refer to still another method, the single alternative vote or preferential vote, which has the merit of determining a majority winner among three or more candidates by a single ballot. Instead of having a series of ballots, eliminating one candidate each time until one remains with an absolute majority, a single ballot is distributed, but on it the electors are required not to place an X opposite one name, but to indicate their first, second, third, etc., choices. Thus if there are three candidates A, B and C, a first choice, say A, would be marked 1, a second choice, say C, marked 2, and B marked 3. When the votes are tallied, first the first-choice votes only, the "1" votes, are counted, and if any candidate receives enough of these to give him a clear majority, i.e., one more than half the total number of votes cast, he is the winner and that is the end of the matter.

If, however, on this first count no candidate secures a majority, the candidate receiving the smallest number of "1" votes is eliminated and all the ballots which show him as first choice are re-examined and the second-choices ("2") on such ballots tabulated. These second choice ("2") votes are then assigned, as designated, to the remaining candidates, who are still in the running, and the process can be repeated, each time eliminating the lowest candidate and re-assigning his votes, until one appears with a clear majority in terms of an accumulation of preferred votes.

The system has the advantage of avoiding multiple balloting, but it does require time and care in the assessment of the ballots.

At a nomination meeting the chairman and secretary normally have the right to vote with the other delegates, although the chairman may decline to do so. The chairman should not participate in discussion after his address at the commencement of proceedings. He must, however, perform all the proper functions of chairmanship, informing the meeting on points of order, preserving decorum, and otherwise ensuring the orderly transaction of the business of the meeting. When improper procedures are taken, instead of ruling them out of order at once he may suggest an alternative means of achieving a desired end.

When resolutions are to be drawn up stating positions or opinions on political, economic or other questions, it is usually expedient to appoint a committee to draft proposals for report to and consideration by a meeting. The report may be dealt with as a whole, but if it contains a number of separate proposals each should be individually discussed, adopted, amended or rejected.

However, it is not essential that resolutions of this kind originate in a committee. Most conventions and assemblies will admit proposals properly introduced as motions by individual members, and they are subject to the same procedure of debate, adoption, amendment or rejection. The procedure on any such occasion is strictly a matter for determination by the body concerned, providing it is not governed by an over-riding parent organization. It is nevertheless important that an adequate body of rules be formulated and that they be rigidly applied.

PART IV

COMPANY MEETINGS

59. General

A limited company or corporation has, under the law, a distinct though in a sense artificial individuality. It can transact business, hold property, sue and be sued, and generally conduct its affairs through its officers and agents, but its activities are in all respects governed by the legal provisions imposed by the charter or other enactment that gave it being.

The principal capital of an incorporated or joint stock company is subscribed by shareholders, who participate in the fortunes of the company only to the extent of the value of their shares from time to time and of the dividends declared by the company. The day to day business of the company is conducted under the supervision of directors elected by the shareholders.

In Canada the power to create an incorporated company is possessed by the federal government and by each of the provinces. The governing statutory provisions in the eleven jurisdictions are similar, but there are differences in detail from one to another. In each jurisdiction a company may be established under the prevailing companies' act or by special statute. There are, moreover, separate statutes applicable to a number of operations, such as banks, railways, insurance, trust and loan companies, etc., and a variety of conditions are available for application in the cases of companies being formed for restricted or special purposes.

General or shareholders' meetings and meetings of boards of directors are held in conformity with all the legal provisions contained in the instrument which gave the company its existence and with by-laws adopted under the authority granted by such instrument. The following material dealing with the conduct of company meetings, while having general application, must therefore be considered with due regard for such regulations and special conditions as may apply in individual cases.

60. By-Laws

The internal management of a corporation or joint stock company is governed by formal regulations known as by-laws. These are usually formulated in the early stages of a company's existence, and they may be added to, amended or withdrawn thereafter as occasion demands. The initiation of by-laws is usually in the board of directors as a part of the performance of the latter's proper function, but by-laws so enacted are subject to confirmation by the shareholders. While they stand on record, by-laws constitute a permanent, continuing rule of action in the conduct of the company's affairs, and in this respect they contrast with resolutions, which may be passed from time to time to meet immediate situations.

Because they must not contravene the laws of the country, must be consonant with the charter or act under which the company acts, and must convey a legally exact intent, it is expedient that by-laws be formulated under legal supervision. Among the important conditions regulated in by-laws are those having to do with the issue of shares and share certificates, the qualifications and remuneration of directors, the appointment of officers and agents of the company, the declaration of dividends, the time and place for the holding of the annual meeting of the company and any other regular or special meeting of the directors or the shareholders, and in general such things as may directly bear on the company's policies and the administration thereof.

61. Directors

The shareholders of a joint stock company in general session elect the directors, whose business it is to administer the affairs of the company, as agents of the shareholders, under the act or charter of incorporation. Until a permanent organization is effected and directors are regularly elected at a general meeting, the persons named as first directors in the charter or statute establishing the company temporarily manage its affairs. They should, however, as soon as practicable, summon a general meeting for the election of directors.

To qualify for directorship an individual is usually required under the charter or by-laws to own shares in the company to a requisite amount, or to be an officer or director of another company owning such shares.

Directors are usually elected annually for a period of one year and if otherwise qualified are eligible for re-election. It is normally provided that vacancies in a board of directors may be filled for an unexpired term by the board from among qualifying shareholders. Most jurisdictions specify that there shall be not less than three directors; unless otherwise provided the number may vary and may be increased or decreased as the need appears, above this minimum.

The directors must act and vote as a board, and a decision made by the board at a duly constituted meeting binds the board and the company, assuming that it acts within its legal powers. An individual director has no authority to act as an agent of the company unless specific powers have been delegated to him, and he may not act or vote by proxy. A majority of the board constitutes a quorum. When the board is large, most jurisdictions authorize the appointment of an executive committee, which performs such functions as may be assigned and is subject to such regulations as may be imposed by the directors.

The directors may enact by-laws, subject in most cases to endorsement by the shareholders, and it is their duty to ensure compliance with them. They elect the company's president, and usually possess the power to hire and discharge the senior members of the company's administrative staff. They are required to inform the shareholders of any serious deficiencies in the company's capital structure and of remedies which they propose to apply. Directors of public companies are forbidden from employing inside knowledge of their affairs to speculate in their shares for private gain, and they are expected to refrain from any engagement or activity which may be considered at variance with the interests of the companies they serve. A director having a personal interest in a proceeding under consideration by the board must make full disclosure and abstain from the matter's discussion.

62. Meetings of Directors

The business of a board of directors must be transacted at a regularly constituted meeting; that is, one of which due notice has been given and at which there is a quorum present. If meetings are regularly held at a specific place, day and time, one notice to that effect may suffice, but a separate notice must be given of any special meeting. The president should preside, or in his absence a vice-president, or the chairman of the board if such a designation is included among the company's officers.

The rules of procedure to be observed are similar to those applicable in an ordinary meeting for the transaction of business, although if the group is small a degree of informality in discussion is commonly allowed. An order of business or agenda should always be prepared, and it may be entered on the left-hand page of the minute book, with a notation by the chairman on the opposite page of the determination of the meeting on each proceeding. The items should be dealt with sequentially and the decisions on all significant issues should be on motion duly seconded and carried by a majority. The secretary keeps a record of all proceedings and both he and the chairman initial all resolutions upon their adoption so that they become identifiable as a dated record of the action taken. A resolution so identified may be incorporated as a part of the minute and hence become a permanent record. A quorum must be maintained throughout the meeting and any by-law or resolution adopted in the absence of a quorum is void. Directors who have declared a personal interest in a matter under discussion cannot be included in the determination of a quorum.

The first meeting of the directors of a newly-formed company will concern itself with matters of organization. It will elect a chairman, appoint a secretary, adopt a common seal, arrange for legal, banking, auditing and other necessary services, appoint a committee to frame regulations, consider the renting of permanent premises, consider a prospectus and share applications, and deal with such other matters as may need to be determined in creating a sound structure for operations.

The following meeting will pursue any questions not fully disposed of at the initial meeting and consider such others as may require attention. Thereafter the meetings of the directors will follow a pattern devised to serve best the purposes of the company, always including the bringing forward of business unfinished at an earlier meeting and provision for the reports of officers or committees which may have been requested at such earlier meeting. It will be a continuing function of the directors to review the financial position of the company, approve its fiscal policies, authorize significant monetary transactions, and take all such actions as may from time to time be necessary with respect to the movement of the company's shares.

63. Shareholders' Meetings

All holders of shares in a company are entitled to receive notice of shareholders' meetings and to participate in and vote at such meetings. The secretary or other officer appointed for the purpose must keep a record of share ownership to ensure that this prerogative is properly exercised. A company's charter or by-laws will provide for the holding of an annual general meeting of the shareholders and may also provide for other interim general meetings. The directors are required to convene a special general meeting to secure the shareholders' sanction of proposed major changes in the company's financial or administrative structure; they will commonly do so to obtain confirmation of a by-law they have enacted or revised or if other conditions arise deemed to require a consensus. In addition, companies' acts provide that the holders of a stipulated proportion of the company's shares may requisition the holding of a special general meeting when in their joint opinion conditions arise to warrant an opportunity being afforded for the expression of the shareholders' views, or to secure a report of the directors on the conduct of the company's business.

(a) Notice of Shareholders' Meetings

Notification of the holding of a general meeting must be given in accordance with the governing legislation or with by-laws enacted in conformity with such legislation. Every shareholder entitled to be present at the meeting must be notified of the time and place of the meeting and the nature of the business to be transacted. Notices are ordinarily despatched by registered mail not less than fourteen days in advance of the date of the meeting. In certain cases it is required that the meeting also be advertised in daily newspapers.

Observance of all of the conditions pertaining to the calling of a meeting is of importance, as the proceedings may be invalidated if they are not observed.

Notices are ordinarily signed by the secretary by order of the board of directors, and they may be accompanied by an instrument of proxy for use by a shareholder who may be unable to attend the meeting in person. It is common and good practice also to include with the notice substantial information concerning important or complicated questions that are to be dealt with, in order that they may receive due prior consideration.

Unless the by-laws of the company otherwise provide, notice is not required of an adjourned meeting, as it is held to be the continuation of the original meeting. However, the business of the adjourned meeting must be only that left unfinished at the original meeting unless there has been interim notice of intention to introduce new business.

(b) *Quorum*

The number to constitute a quorum at shareholders' meetings normally will be fixed by by-law and will be influenced by the total number of shareholders; when the number is small more than half may be required and as the number increases the proportion will be reduced. In some cases a quorum may be related to the number of shares held rather than to individuals as such.

In the absence of a quorum a meeting cannot proceed, but the by-laws or articles ordinarily provide that the meeting may be adjourned. Lacking such a provision, and in the absence of a quorum, the meeting will lapse.

The register of shareholders should always be available to the chairman and secretary at a general meeting, ordinary or special, in case any question arises regarding qualification to attend or a quorum, or a poll is to be taken based on share ownership.

(c) *Proxies*

The term proxy is used to denote the function of a deputy who acts as a substitute for another, or the authority or power to so act, or the document giving such authorization.

Most governing acts or by-laws provide that a shareholder may be represented at a general meeting by a proxy, but require that the proxy himself be fully qualified to vote in his own right. The proxy is thus entitled to exercise his own vote and that of the shareholder by whom he was appointed. A properly executed form or instrument of proxy is required, and it is subject to scrutiny by the secretary and to judgement as to its validity by the chairman. Alternate proxies may be named in a single proxy form: "A" or in his absence "B," etc. A proxy may be appointed for a specified meeting or to act until his authorization is revoked or replaced or until it is invalidated by the personal attendance of the appointer.

The following is a form of proxy:

The undersigned, being a holder of (number) shares of (company), hereby appoints and authorizes (name) of the city of (name) to vote for him and on his behalf at the meeting of the company to be held (day, month and year) and at any adjournment thereof.

(date & signature of shareholder.)

(d) *Chairmanship*

Ordinarily the by-laws or articles of a company provide that the president or, in his absence, a vice-president or other officer shall take the Chair at meetings. When there is no such provision the shareholders may elect a chairman from their own number.

The duties of a chairman are regulated by both law and custom. The chairman must assure the legality of the notice of the meeting and the regularity of all motions and amendments thereto. He is authorized to decide all procedural questions which may arise requiring immediate decision, to call for votes and announce results. It is his duty to follow the agenda and call the items of business in order, to receive motions, ensure that they are seconded, and submit them to the meeting for discussion. He must insist that discussion be relevant to the issue under consideration, and that any amendments introduced are properly related to the motions they seek to modify.

With the approval of the meeting, the chairman may terminate discussion on any question and call for a vote thereon. When the scheduled business is completed, he asks whether there is any other business to be considered and rules whether an attempt to introduce new business is in order. He terminates the meeting when all of the purposes for which it was called have been fulfilled.

(e) *Procedure*

Having satisfied himself of the presence of a quorum, the chairman will call the meeting to order; the secretary will then read the notice calling the meeting and certify that it was mailed to the shareholders in accordance with any governing provisions. Scrutineers may be appointed to attest the number of shareholders represented in person or by proxy. The minutes of the last meeting are read and, if necessary, corrected, and are signed by the presiding officer as correct. The business of the meeting will then be transacted in the order in which the various items appear in a prepared agenda. These items will generally include financial statements and an auditor's report, a formal report of the directors, and a statement by the president on the company's current operating position, frequently in relation to general market and economic conditions. The various reports may be approved and adopted individually on motion, or they may be grouped for approval in one inclusive motion. At an annual general meeting directors will be elected, usually by ballot, and auditors appointed.

If proposals are introduced for the shareholders' approval, they should be in written form and be presented with a motion for adoption. If they are in general terms they may be debated and they are subject to amendment in accordance with normal practice. However, if a proposal is introduced on a matter of substance in specific terms, and the shareholders have been informed of these terms, it must be presented as formulated and either approved or rejected without amendment. The only permissible modification in these circumstances would be of wording to clarify, without altering, the intent.

The chairman has no authority to conclude or adjourn a meeting at his own pleasure before the business set down for consideration has been completed, unless there is a provision in the by-laws or articles empowering him to do so. Should he be so empowered, however, he cannot be overruled by the majority.

(f) *Voting*

The by-laws of every company should include regulations relative to the voting at shareholders meetings.

The Companies Act of Canada provides that in the absence of other provisions in the letters patent, supplementary letters patent, or by-laws of the company, every shareholder is entitled to one vote for each share then held by him; such votes may be cast in person or by proxy, if the proxy is himself a shareholder, but no shareholder in arrears of a call on his shares, that is, who has failed to honour a demand for an additional deposit on securities he has bought on margin, is entitled to vote at any meeting. All questions are to be determined by the majority of votes, the chairman to have a casting vote in case of an equality of votes.

In the transaction of the ordinary business of a meeting the shareholders will record their vote in the usual way, by a show of hands, without regard for the number of shares held. Any shareholder may demand that a poll be taken, however, and unless provided for in regulations the manner of conducting the poll is determined by the chairman. Issues of substance should always be decided by poll, thereby assuring a conclusion based upon majority share representation.

In conducting a poll, each shareholder is supplied with a ballot which he marks either for or against the resolution under consideration and signs. Scrutineers appointed prior to the taking of the poll then note on each ballot the number of shares held in person or represented by proxy by the person signing the ballot. The votes should be totalled in terms of shares, for and against the resolution, only after all of the ballots have been cast; no attempt should be made to record a person's vote as he deposits his ballot. The scrutineers report their finding to the chairman, who announces the result. Regulations generally provide that the chairman is entitled to vote as an ordinary member, but he must do so while the poll is in progress and before the tendency of the vote is evident. He may, however, give a second or casting vote in the case of an equality of votes.

Unless clearly prohibited by statute or regulations, a poll may be demanded on any question under consideration even if there has been a show of hands on that question. Nevertheless, the chairman is not bound to grant a poll unless it is demanded in accordance with the regulations, and in granting a poll he may fix the time and place of its taking. It may be expedient to take the poll immediately, or at the conclusion of the meeting when all other business has been transacted, or sometimes in the case of large companies with numerous shareholders it may be deferred until a later time, which the chairman will designate. In all cases the chairman must be governed in his decision by any applicable by-laws or regulations; in the absence of such directive he will rule on the basis of the circumstances that prevail and his own discretion.

64. Minutes

The law requires that every company shall cause minutes of all proceedings at meetings of the shareholders and of the directors and of any executive committee to be entered in books kept for that purpose, and the articles or by-laws of every company should so provide. It is normally the responsibility of the secretary to record proceedings while the meeting is in progress, under the direction of the chairman, and to prepare the full minutes as soon as possible thereafter. They may then be submitted for approval at the next meeting and when approved and signed by the chairman they become *prima facie* evidence of the proceedings. The minutes hence possess a distinct legal significance; they constitute, moreover, a complete record of transactions which are of substantial value for subsequent reference. In this respect it is advisable that they be indexed.

The minutes should record the place, date and time of the meeting and should provide evidence that all governing acts and by-laws, including notice, have been complied with. The chairman and secretary should be named, and those in attendance listed, at least to the extent of showing the presence of a quorum. The minutes should contain the full text of every resolution considered and state its disposition. The names of proposers and seconders of motions, or of those who voted for and against, need not be recorded, but a request of a member that his dissent be recorded should be complied with. Reports or other documents presented at a meeting may be incorporated in the minutes as an appendix, with a suitable reference in the body of the minutes themselves, or they may be referred to as filed. The details of contracts or other matters involving finance should be fully recorded in the minutes.

Every precaution should be taken to avoid any impression of the minutes having been altered after their approval. If a correction is necessary when they are submitted for approval, the correction should be handwritten at once and initialled by the chairman. A decision made and duly recorded in the minutes may not be altered except by a new resolution rescinding the former one. To preserve the integrity of the minutes, they should be kept in a solid binder under the strict control of the secretary, with the pages consecutively numbered.

Directors always possess the right of access to the minutes or any other company records and documents. Shareholders are usually permitted to examine the minutes of shareholders' meetings, but not those of meetings of the board of directors.

65. Company Books

Companies are required, by the legislation under which they are incorporated, to maintain certain books and records. It is ordinar-

92

ily provided that these shall include (1) a copy of the letters patent and of any supplementary letters patent issued to the company and of the memorandum of agreement and of all by-laws of the company; (2) the names, alphabetically arranged, of all persons who are or have been shareholders of the company; (3) the address and calling of every such person, while a shareholder, as far as can be ascertained; (4) the names, addresses and callings of all persons who are or have been directors of the company with the several dates at which each became or ceased to be a director; (5) the number of shares of each class held by each shareholder; (6) the amounts paid in and remaining unpaid, respectively, on the shares of each shareholder; (7) the minutes of all proceedings at meetings of the shareholders and of the directors and of any executive committee; (8) all sums of money received and expended by the company and the matters in respect of which the receipt and expenditure take place; (9) all sales and purchases by the company; (10) the assets and liabilities of the company; (11) all other transactions affecting the financial position of the company.

The books are normally to be kept at the head office of the company and are to be open to shareholders and creditors of the company, or their qualified representatives, during usual business hours.

Part V

SOME ILLUSTRATIONS

Suspension of Rules

Chairman: Will the meeting please come to order? Ladies and gentlemen, as you are aware, this meeting has been called somewhat hurriedly, as we face a deadline for the completion of certain arrangements in connection with our Association's investments. It was not possible to give the required ten days notice of the meeting, as specified in our by-laws, and our first action must therefore be to suspend, for the purposes of this meeting only, that requirement, as set out in Article III, Section 2.

Member 1: I move that for the purposes of this meeting the ten day notice requirement be suspended.

Member 2: Second.

Chairman: Are any opposed? No. I therefore declare this meeting duly called and regularly constituted.

Minutes

Chairman: The first order of business is the confirmation of minutes. Mr. Secretary, will you please read the minutes of the last meeting?

(The Secretary does so.)

Chairman: Do you find the minutes in order? If so, may I have a motion for their adoption?

Member 1: Mr. Chairman, I believe there is one error. Mr. A. was named a member of the nominating committee but in the minutes he is not included with the others as comprising that committee.

Chairman: Thank you, you are quite right. Do all agree? Mr. Secretary, please make that correction.

With that correction, do you now find the minutes a true record?

Member 1: I move that the minutes of the last meeting as corrected be approved and confirmed.

Member 2: Second.

Chairman: All in favour? Thank you. The next order of business is . . .

Report of Committee

. . . a report of our Committee on finances. Mr. B., as chairman of that Committee, will you kindly submit your report?

(Mr. B. does so.)

Chairman: Ladies and gentlemen, you have heard the report. Is there any comment?

Alternative I

Member 1: I move that the report of the Committee on Finances be received.

Chairman: If there is no further comment . . . (pause) . . . the report is received and it will be filed in our records.

Alternative II

Member 1: Mr. Chairman, in my view there is some confusion of the data contained in Part 2 of the report. May I suggest that instead of . . . (explains his point).

Chairman: Do you agree, Mr. B?

(There is discussion of the point.)

Chairman: We seem to be agreed that the report would be clarified by the revision suggested. Is the report acceptable as so revised?

Member 1: I move that the report of the Committee on Finances, as revised, be adopted.

Member 2: I second the motion.

Chairman: It has been moved and seconded that the report of the Committee on Finances, as revised, be adopted. All in favour? . . . Are any opposed? . . . Thank you. The motion carries.

Alternative III

Member 1: Mr. Chairman, in my view Section 2 of the report is very confusing and it contains inadequate data to support the conclusions reached. Would it be in order to request the committee to amplify this part of its report and re-submit it to our next meeting?

Chairman: Your proposal is in order provided it bears the support of other members. What is the opinion of the meeting?

Member 2: Mr. Chairman, I agree. I move that the report be referred back to the committee for substantial amplification of Section 2 and re-submission at our next meeting.

Member 3: I second the motion.

Chairman: It has been moved and seconded that the report of the

Member 2: I believe that we have something to say in this matter, Mr. Chairman. I move that a brief be prepared and that it be submitted on our behalf.

Member 3: I second that motion.

Chairman: It has been moved and seconded that a brief be prepared and submitted to the Commission on Energy Resources on behalf of our association. The matter is open for discussion.

(An orderly debate follows.)

Member 4: Mr. Chairman, it is obvious that much work must be done in the preparation of the brief in question. I move to amend the motion by providing that a special committee be appointed by the Chairman to study the whole matter and prepare a draft brief for our approval.

Member 5: I second the motion to amend.

Chairman: You have heard the proposed amendment. Is there any comment?

(The proposed amendment is discussed.)

Member 6: Mr. Chairman, we are under some pressure of time. I move a subamendment that the committee's draft brief be submitted for our approval not later than our next regular monthly meeting.

Member 7: Second.

Chairman: You have heard the amendment. Is there further discussion?

(There is none.)

Chairman: The question is as follows: It is moved that a brief be prepared and submitted to the Commission on Energy Resources on behalf of our association; by amendment it is moved that a committee be appointed by the Chairman to study the whole question and prepare a draft brief for our approval; by subamendment it is moved that the draft brief be submitted for our approval not later than our next monthly meeting.

Member 8: Mr. Chairman, I move that we engage expert assistance in the preparation of our brief.

Chairman: Mr. 8, we have before us a main motion and two amendments. At this point your motion is not in order.

I shall now put the question. Those in favour of the amendment in amendment please signify. (There is a show of hands.) ... Those opposed? (There are none.) Those in favour of the amendment as amended, please signify. (Again a show of hands and none opposed.) Shall the main motion as amended carry? (A show of hands.) Are any opposed? ... (One hand rises, indicating that there is one opponent of the principle embodied in the main motion.) ... The motion carries.

Member B: Mr. Chairman, I should like my negative vote to be recorded.

Chairman: Mr. Secretary, please record Mr. B.'s negative vote in the minutes.

Postponement of Action on Motion

(In the following examples a main motion is before the meeting and debate is in progress.)

Alternative I

Member 1: (rising and securing attention of Chairman) Mr. Chairman, I move that the debate be adjourned.

Chairman: Is there a seconder for the motion that the debate be adjourned?

Member 2: I second the motion.

Member 3. Mr. Chairman, I object. It seems to me that. ...

Chairman: Mr. 3., I am sorry, you are out of order. A motion to adjourn is not debatable. It has been moved and seconded that the debate on the motion that (states the motion) be adjourned. All in favour? ... Those opposed? ... The motion carries. The next order of business is. ...

(If the motion to adjourn is defeated the debate on the main motion continues as though there had been no intervention.)

Alternative II

Member 1: Mr. Chairman I move that we proceed to the next order of business.

Member 2: I second the motion.

Chairman: It has been moved and seconded that we proceed to the next order of business. Those in favour? ... Those opposed? ... The motion is lost. Debate will proceed on the main motion before us, which is ...

(If the motion had carried the chairman would have at once proceeded to the next item on the agenda. The suspended motion could, however, be revived at a subsequent meeting.)

Alternative III ("the previous question")

Member 1: Mr. Chairman, I move that the question be now put.

Member 2: I second the motion.

Chairman: It has been moved and seconded that the question be now put. Is there any discussion?

(The motion is debatable, but debate must be confined to this motion; it may not at this point extend to the main motion to which it refers.)

Chairman: Is it your pleasure that the question be now put? Those in favour? . . . Those opposed? . . . The motion carries. I shall now put the question (the main motion) which is as follows . . .

OR

The motion is lost. In consequence the question may *not* be now put. The next order of business is . . .

(Again, a question so set aside may be re-introduced at a subsequent meeting.)

Alternative IV

Member 1: Mr. Chairman, in my view this question demands much more investigation than we can give it in our full meeting this evening. I therefore move that it be referred to our Committee on Procedures for study and report.

Member 2: I agree and second the motion.

Chairman: It has been moved and seconded that the question before us, namely (briefly states the question) be referred to our Committee on Procedure for study and report. Is there any discussion?

Member 3: Yes, Mr. Chairman. In view of the monetary considerations involved, I move to amend the motion to refer by adding the words 'in consultation with the Committee on Finance' after the words 'Committee on Procedure.'

Member 2: I second the motion to amend.

Chairman: It has been moved and seconded to amend the motion to refer by adding the words 'in consultation with the Committee on Finance.' Is there discussion of the proposed amendment? . . . If not, those in favour of the amendment please signify. . . . Those opposed? . . . The amendment carries. The motion to refer as amended is therefore as follows: (states the motion). Is there further discussion? . . . Those in favour? . . . Opposed? . . . The motion carries. The question before us, namely that (states *main* motion) is therefore referred. The next order of business is . . .

Notice of Motion

Chairman: The next order of business is a notice of motion to amend the by-laws of our Association. Mr. A., please.

Mr. A: Yes, Mr. Chairman. I give notice that at the next or a sub-sequent meeting I will introduce a motion to amend the by-laws of the Association to the following effect: (he may provide full details of the amendment he will propose, or may merely summarize their intent on the understanding that members will be supplied with full details prior to the meeting at which they will be considered.)

Member: Mr. Chairman, it seems to me that the change in the by-laws suggested will be counter-productive. They will . . .

Chairman: Mr. B., discussion at this stage is not in order. There will be full opportunity to debate the proposed changes when a formal amending motion is introduced. The next order of business is . . .

Order

(A motion is before the meeting and debate is in progress.)

Member A: (interrupting speaker) Mr. Chairman, on a point of order, the speaker is extending his remarks beyond the question under consideration; they apply to another subject which arises as a separate item later in today's agenda.

Chairman: Your point is well taken, Mr. A. Mr. B., please confine your remarks to the question before us, which is . . . (states gist of motion).

OR

Chairman: I disagree, Mr. A. In my view Mr. B.'s remarks are relevant to the question under discussion, and I so rule.

Member 1: I appeal from the ruling of the Chair.

Member 2: I second the appeal.

Chairman: The ruling of the Chair regarding the relevancy or propriety of Mr. B.'s remarks is appealed. Shall the Chair's ruling be sustained?

Those in favour? . . . Those opposed? . . . The ruling of the Chair is sustained. Please continue, Mr. B.

(Should the ruling not be sustained, the chairman must request Mr. B. to confine his remarks strictly to the question, and must see that he does so by repeated admonition if necessary.)

Mr. B: I resent these repeated interruptions . . . (uses intemperate language).

Chairman: Order, please.

Mr. B: I do not propose to be dictated to by . . . (more intemperate language).

Chairman: Order, please. Mr. B., I must ask you to conform to the rules and to the usual proprieties. Unless you are prepared to do so I must ask you to resume your seat and I shall call upon another speaker.

> (The meeting proceeds, but is later distracted by conversations between members.)

Chairman: Excuse me, Mr. B. Ladies and gentlemen, I call for order. Please give the speaker the courtesy of your attention. If there is any interruption of these proceedings that can properly be made – and by properly I mean in conformity with parliamentary usage – the point can be made only to the Chair, when it will be dealt with in accordance with that usage. Please proceed, Mr. B.

> (Repeated efforts to maintain order fail.)

Chairman: Ladies and gentlemen, this meeting cannot proceed without order. We seem to have arrived at a point of failure in the maintenance of order. I shall therefore recess the meeting for twenty minutes. We shall re-convene at three-thirty and resume our discussion at the point at which it has been broken off. (Leaves the Chair.)

Privilege

> (Debate is in progress.)

Member: (interrupts speaker) Mr. Chairman, I rise on a point of privilege. The speaker has attributed to me remarks that I did not in fact make, implying . . . (explains his point).

Chairman: Mr. B., you have heard Mr. A.'s point. I think we should pause for a moment for clarification.

> (An opportunity is provided for rectifying a misunderstanding, and for Mr. A. to establish that he did not make the remarks attributed to him.)

Chairman: Does that clear your point, Mr. A?

Mr. A: Yes, Mr. Chairman, thank you.

Chairman: Mr. B., please proceed.

Form of Minutes

Minutes of a meeting of the Alpha Zeta Society held at the Royal York Hotel, Toronto, on Wednesday, 10 March, 1976, called to order at 2.30 p.m.

Present: Messrs A. B. Cowan, D. Edwards, F. G. Howard, Isaac Jones, K. Lambert, Maynard Noakes, O. P. Quayle, Reginald Soward, T. U. Vernon, Wm. Yates.

Also attending by invitation: Messrs A. B. Chadwick and Donald Ewing.

The President, Mr. Lambert, in the Chair

The Chairman introduced and welcomed Messrs Chadwick and Ewing, who were attending as representatives of the Calgary Branch.

Minutes

The minutes of the last meeting, held 11 February 1976, were read and confirmed on motion.

Correspondence

Receipt was reported of the following communications:

(a) From the Daily Advertiser, dated 25 February 1976, quoting rates in response to the Society's request.

(b) From Mr. Frank Gower, dated 16 February 1976, submitting his resignation due to his transfer to a new post in Halifax.

It was agreed: re (a) to refer the matter of an advertising program to the Publicity Committee for consideration and report; re (b) to accept the resignation with regret.

Relations with Calgary Branch

At the Chairman's request Messrs Chadwick and Ewing described the recent activities of the Calgary Branch, with particular reference to representations recently made to provincial authorities in the matter of licensing regulations. The representations had not led to a satisfactory outcome. They suggested a new approach jointly by representatives of the Society's various branches to create a more impressive impact.

The matter was discussed at some length, whereupon it was unanimously agreed, on motion duly seconded, that representatives of each of the Society's five Branches should be requested to meet to determine a program of concerted action.

The Chairman was authorized to take such action as might be necessary to give effect to this decision.

The Chairman thanked Messrs Chadwick and Ewing for their attendance, and they withdrew.

Financial Report

A report of the Committee on Finances for the period ended 29 February 1976 was received and approved. (Copy attached.)

Concern was expressed over the increasing disparity between receipts and expenditures, and an improved effort to recover dues now in arrears was advocated.

Proposed Submission to Commission on Energy Resources
The Chairman having introduced the question of a proposed submission by this Society to the Commission on Energy Resources, it was duly moved that a brief be prepared and submitted.

In the course of debate an amendment was offered that a special committee be appointed by the Chairman to study the whole matter and prepare a draft brief for approval. In further debate a subamendment was offered that the proposed draft brief of the committee be submitted for approval not later than the Society's next monthly meeting.

The questions being put and the amendments carried, the motion as amended was adopted. It was thereby resolved:

> That a brief be prepared and submitted on the Society's behalf to the Commission on Energy Resources; that a committee be appointed by the Chairman to study the whole matter and prepare a draft brief for approval, and that the draft brief in question be submitted for approval not later than the Society's next monthly meeting.

One member, Mr. Wm. Yates, dissented from the decision.

Annual Meeting
The Chairman reported that in conformity with the provisions of the by-laws the Society's annual meeting would be held in the month of May. Suitable arrangements for the meeting were being made by the Executive Committee, with a tentative date of Thursday, May 27. Notification would be directed by mail to all members.

There being no further business the Chairman then closed the meeting.

Minutes confirmed_____ Secretary_____

Form of Report
Pursuant to a resolution adopted at a meeting of the Society held March 10, 1976, the following were appointed as a committee to prepare a draft brief for submission to the commission on Energy Resources: Messrs A. B. Cowan (chairman), D. Edwards, Frederick Gower, H. I. Jones, and the President *ex officio*. The committee has met on a number of occasions. It has examined the terms of reference of the Commission on Energy Resources and has reviewed the policies of our Society that appear relevant thereto. It

is the committee's opinion that . . . (general statement of relevant considerations, etc.)

The Committee therefore recommends:

(a) That a brief in the terms of a draft attached hereto be submitted to the Commission on Energy Resources.

(b) That the submission be made by the President of the Society, accompanied by such other members as he may name, at a time, and place to be arranged.

(c) That copies of the brief be released to the news media immediately following its formal submission.

> Respectfully submitted,
> (signed) Alfred Cowan
> Chairman

(If the report is adopted in general meeting without change, each of its recommendations must be acted upon. It and the accompanying draft brief are, however, subject to revision at such general meeting and final action is then determined on the basis of the revisions. All revisions should be explicitly recorded in the minutes.)

Form of Minutes of Company Meetings
Board of Directors

Epsilon Company Limited

Meeting of Board of Directors held at the Company's Head Office, 111 King Street West, Toronto, on Monday, 9 February 1976, at 10.30 a.m.

Present: Directors Allan Brown, C. D. Evans, Frank G. Head. Leave of Absence: I. Janes and P. Q. Raven. Also attending: the General Manager, Noah Oates, and Secretary, K. L. Moon.

Mr. Allan Brown, President, in the Chair.

Notice

Proof of service of notice of meeting was filed by the Secretary.

Minutes

The minutes of the last meeting of the Directors, held 5 January 1976, were read and approved and were ordered to be signed as correct.

Statement of Finances

A statement of finances for the six-month period ended 31 December 1975 was reviewed and approved.

Contract with Gamma Corporation

A draft contract with the Gamma Corporation was reviewed and, subject to minor adjustment, its execution by the President was authorized on motion.

Communication from Delta Associates

A communication addressed to the Company by Messrs Delta Associates, dated 31 January 1976, was read. The Directors being of the opinion that ... etc., the Secretary was directed to reply accordingly.

Annual Meeting

To comply with the provisions of the by-laws it was, on motion duly seconded, unanimously resolved:

That the annual meeting of shareholders of the Company be held at the Head Office of the Company on Wednesday, 31 March 1976, at 2.30 p.m.

There being no further business the meeting terminated.

Minutes confirmed_____   President_____

                                     Secretary_____

Meeting of Shareholders

Minutes of a special general meeting of the shareholders of the Epsilon Company Limited held at the Head Office of the Company, 111 King Street West, Toronto, on Tuesday, 21 October 1975, at 2:30 p.m. Present: Messrs Alfred Brown, C. D. Evans, Frank G. Head, I. Janes, ... (and others).

Mr. Alfred Brown, President, in the Chair.

Scrutineers

The Chairman appointed Messrs N. O. Percy, Q. Rance and S. T. Umial as scrutineers to report on the number of shares represented and on any poll taken at this meeting.

Quorum

A quorum of the shareholders having been found by the scrutineers, either in person or by proxy, the Chairman declared the meeting validly constituted.

Notice

The notice convoking the meeting was read by the Secretary who filed with the Chairman a certificate proving mailing of notice to the shareholders. Proof of service was ordered appended to the minutes of this day's meeting.

Minutes

The minutes of the special general meeting held 12 February 1975 were read by the Secretary and were approved on motion.

Report of Directors

It was resolved unanimously that the report of the Directors and the accounts annexed thereto, having been distributed, be taken as read, and upon motion duly seconded it was resolved that such report and accounts be, and they are hereby, adopted.

Election of Director

Upon motion duly seconded and carried unanimously Mr. A. B. Currie was elected to the Board of Directors in the place of Mr. E. F. Ghent, retired.

Administrative Policy

It was moved by Mr. Smith, seconded by Mr. Phillips:

> That . . . (the actual terms of a specific motion relating to administrative policy, details of which have been supplied to the shareholders in advance of the meeting).

It was moved in amendment by Mr. Archer seconded by Mr. Brown:

> That the action proposed be deferred pending the appointment of a committee of five shareholders, with power to add to their number, to enquire into the administrative structure and management experience of the Company, such committee being authorized to call for books and documents and to obtain such legal and other assistance as may be necessary and to report to a special general meeting of shareholders to be held not later than 31 January 1976.

On a show of hands the Chairman declared the amendment lost.

A poll was then demanded and taken and showed _____ votes for the amendment and _____ votes opposed. (A report of the scrutineers, if any, may be entered in the minutes.) The Chairman declared the amending motion lost. The question then being put on the main motion, it was resolved in the affirmative.

There being no further business the Chairman declared the meeting terminated.

Minutes confirmed_____   President_____

                                     Secretary_____

Index

(References are to page numbers)

110

112